Love
Shrinks

Other titles by Sharyn Wolf

Fifty Ways to Find a Lover

Guerilla Dating Tactics

How to Stay Lovers for Life

So You Want to Get Married

This Old Spouse

a memoir of a
marriage counselor's
divorce

Love
Shrinks

SHARYN WOLF

SOHO

Published by
Soho Press, Inc.
853 Broadway
New York, NY 10003

Library of Congress Cataloging-in-Publication Data

Wolf, Sharyn.
Love shrinks : a memoir of a marriage counselor's divorce /
Sharyn Wolf.
    p. cm.
ISBN 978-1-56947-936-0
1. Wolf, Sharyn. 2. Divorced women—United States—Biography.
3. Marriage counselors—United States—Biography. 4. Divorce—
United States. 5. MarriageUnited States. I. Title.
HQ834.W668 2011
306.89'3092—dc22
[B]   2010045586

Printed in the United States of America

10 9 8 7 6 4 5 3 2 1

For Karen Armstrong

Contents

Acknowledgments

I want to thank Charles Salzberg and Ross Klavan, Jennifer La Pierre, Debra Wolf, Ian Mackler, Michelle Wolf, David Sparr, Laura Vladimirova, Lynn Kwalwasser, Katharine Butler and Tom Wolbarst for reading drafts of this book along the way and offering their generous support. Thanks to my agent, Helen Zimmerman, for taking on this book and seeing me through. Thanks to Jen Greenberg for the photo. I want to thank Victoria Watson, C.J. Jadusingh, Michelle Hyde, Norma Rubin, Milton Rubin and Chris Nee for their kindness during this process. Thanks to The Jazz Foundaton of America for letting me be part of their valuable work. I was very lucky to have Bronwen Hruska and Juliet Grames as my editors. They were a dream to work with, and they made this a better book. Thanks to Amy King for her amazing cover design, Justin Hargett for his hard work handling the publicity and Ailen Lujo for her marketing wizardry. In the end, I especially want to thank my patients. They healed me.

"Is love the reward, or the test itself?"

WILLIAM MATTHEWS

Introduction

*T*his is the story of a marriage counselor who couldn't keep her own marriage together. She had loved her husband in the past, and still did love parts of him. She tried everything she could think of to make their fifteen years together work: individual counseling, couple's counseling, group therapy, self-help books, pretending everything was fine, anti-depressant medication, waiting, praying, pretending everything was fine.

Meanwhile, as all these solutions were failing her, the marriage counselor wrote books: *50 Ways to Find a Lover, Guerrilla Dating Tactics, How to Stay Lovers for Life, So You Want to Get Married,* and *This Old Spouse.* She made eight appearances on *Oprah,* and on hundreds of radio and television programs. She led seminars with titles like *72 Ways to Flirt.*

As the marriage counselor and her husband went without speaking for weeks at a time, Carnation hired her to talk about how cocoa could cure seasonal affective disorder. Procter & Gamble hired her to talk about how Just For Men hair color could revitalize a man's self-esteem and make him sexy again. Oil of Olay hired her to help launch their cosmetic line. A snack manufacturer paid her to explain how preference in pretzel-shape might offer clues to personality and future life choices.

The hot lights did not distract her. The surprise questions did not flummox her. The marriage counselor invented pithy catchphrases under pressure: *The problem is the place you start working*; or *The least you can do is commit as much sweat to happiness as you've committed to keeping crummy relationships together*. She always let the host get the biggest laugh.

She was the redhead who said that love lasts when you think in threes: what's good for you, what's good for your partner, and what's good for the relationship.

But these were not questions the marriage counselor was willing to ask herself.

Or in any case, not willing to answer.

MAYBE IT'S ONLY here, in this love story about divorce, this tribute to the good heart of an ex-husband whom I don't want back, this one-sided account of who failed whom, that I have begun to consider such questions.

And these:

Why are love stories the most painful stories of all? Why didn't I write about *that* in my relationship advice books?

How long should you try before you throw in the towel? I never mentioned that, either.

I wanted to tell people what was going on behind closed doors. I wanted to be the one to get advice and help, but it was my nature to pick a time and place and standard delivery where I would not be taken seriously.

For example, when I met my good friends Charles and Ross for our bimonthly lunch at Grange Hall:

"I want a divorce," I announced as we looked at menus.

"Again?" Charles said at the very same moment Ross said, "From whom?"

"I'm miserable."

"As are we all," Charles intoned, ordering a hamburger. "I'll share my fries," he told Ross.

"I've been miserable for years," I added, ordering a turkey sandwich.

"Did I just hear you say you'd *share* your French fries?" Ross asked Charles.

"WE HAVEN'T HAD SEX SINCE THE CARTER ADMINISTRATION. WE OWE FORTY THOUSAND DOLLARS IN BACK TAXES. I'M ON EVERY ANXIETY MEDICATION IN THE PDR AND A FEW YOU CAN ONLY FIND IN MEXICO!" I yelled out.

"Okay, Okay. I'll share my fries with you, too," Charles replied.

THIS STORY IS true. I know, because I lived every word of it. It is fractured nonfiction, friction or fraction. It is an extended X-ray of the number of heartbeats per heartbreak.

When your marriage is in trouble and you can't decide what to do, friends often ask: Why did you get married in the first place? Why did you stay this long?

Well, terrible marriages have stellar moments, little lifeboats. Also—and I see this in my practice every day—miserable couples are just as attached as happy couples, just as likely to take a bullet for each other. At the end of each chapter in this book, I will tell you one solid reason why I stayed married.

Here, for example, is the first reason I stayed married so long:

When I was in fourth grade, a bus came after school to take the girls who wanted to go to the Girl's Club. We could do activities from three to five—sewing, roller skating, taking a nature class. Then the bus would take us back to school, where our parents could pick us up. I had always wanted to roller-skate.

At the Girl's Club, I watched older, experienced girls glide by in dashy little skirts, twirling in reverie. I knew that I was born to twirl, too. So I was surprised at the sound of my right wrist bone cracking to the beat of the music when I fell down on my first attempt.

With one hand, I unlaced and turned in the skates. I walked to the sewing class, then to the library, then to a spelling bee, then back to the library. I tried not to stay in one place too long.

I was ashamed of having an accident, scared to ask if there was a nurse, terrified of being a burden to the Girl's Club, sure they would be mad at me and not let me come back.

I was nine years old.

When I got home, over dinner, I told my parents that I broke my wrist. My father felt sure that if I'd *really* broken it I would have said something sooner. My mother looked at the swelling carefully. My parents starting fighting about my wrist, and my mother hated to fight. She hated it more than anything.

In the middle of the night she heard me weeping on the bathroom floor. She took me to the emergency room, and I came home in a long white cast.

Girls like me stay in bad relationships because we don't want to upset anyone. My husband was much the same. He was a man who would understand the story of my broken wrist. In a room of hundreds of people, people like us spot each other right away.

I HAVE SET this memoir inside my psychotherapy office, in my old secondhand psychotherapist's chair, with its black-and-white African mud cloth and the pillow for my back; the place where, when I am supposed to listen fully, I occasionally lapse. Lapsing is easy because my office is downstairs from my house, and it was especially easy while I was trying to sort out my marriage, which was hidden on the other side of my office door like Rochester's wife.

This book takes place in multiple time zones, because I live in multiple time zones—I have since I was a little girl. In some ways, we all do. A visit home to your parents makes you feel six again. Falling in love makes you feel sixteen again. Robert Frost accepted the Pulitzer Prize for poetry when he was in his eighties and said, "I wish my mother were here." For me, too, the past and the present are inextricably linked inside my head, like lions caught in a net.

BECAUSE I COULD not tell, I chose a profession that depends on telling.

My patients, whom you will meet in this book, are more than disguised. I may have changed gender, I may have blended five people together, I may have tinkered with a story in any number of ways. I may even have made it all up, and still, I'd be telling you the truth. Their hearts and souls fill these pages. Their true identities do not.

I want to say something about the use of the word "patient." Today the mental health field calls people in psychotherapy all kinds of things—clients, patients, consumers. Several years ago I heard Elie Weisel speaking at a family therapy conference. He said he *wanted* to be called a "patient." He wanted to feel the mystery and the potential that being a patient has to offer. He also wanted psychotherapy practitioners not to be afraid to say we have the power to be a healing force. I realized that if he'd wanted to be a "client," he would have opened a Schwab account.

I want to be a healing force, a Seeing Eye dog, in the reconfiguration of long-term pain. Thus, it was annoying to discover that my own troubles, sprinkled over the years like salt on a wound, my own bad marriage, and my own wild inconsistencies were getting in the way, shoving me back and forth like an unfortunate choice of a ride at the amusement park.

I tried focusing on my patients and putting my life aside. In the end, it didn't work, because the more I focused on my patients, the better they got—which created further evidence that I was lagging behind.

Their lives got unstuck. Mine did not.

They reported that they felt more positive about their relationships. I did not.

They felt happier. I did not.

I couldn't seem to tap in myself what I'd tapped in them.

So, this book is also a thank-you note to those who lay down on my couch and, unknowingly, nudged me forward. Most of the time a patient knows if the therapist is helping her, but she may never know how much she is helping the therapist—or how much the therapist really needs help. Perhaps, then, this book is also a love letter to my patients, who pointed the way.

Sometimes I fantasize that, if I'd had another kind of job, I'd have had another kind of marriage—a weekend house in Pennsylvania, a sturdy retirement fund, perhaps even an exchange student to host for a semester. We'd have been folded into each other in an intricate, unmistakable pattern, a plumped-up quilt, and we'd have stayed together until that day when the very worst and the very best marriages are momentarily indistinguishable—when one spouse buries the other.

Love
Shrinks

chapter 1

I Have a 999-Crane Marriage

My patient Danny has taken up origami. Lately, when I step into my waiting room to invite him into my office, he is bent over like Pinocchio's father, manipulating small, colorful pieces of paper into his expressionistic menagerie. Last week he offered me an exquisitely articulated turtle. Today, he lifted his head to reveal a psychedelic crane.

Danny visits me because he is sad. His girlfriend of eight years lives seven thousand miles away in another country. She lives with her mother, who never wants her to leave. The girlfriend keeps telling him she's coming here to marry him and make babies, yet she keeps postponing the date and failing to fill out her fiancée visa. Once, it was because her mother got too nervous. Another time, it was because of a job transfer. And yet another time, it was because the last solar eclipse of the century made the sky so dark that no crane could find its way.

I interpret Danny's animals. If she will not fly to him, will he fly to her? Which one of them is the *real* turtle?

He tells me the Japanese say that if you make a thousand origami cranes, your wish will come true. In Japan, a young girl named Sadako Sasaki was very sick, so she began to make cranes. Day after day, she folded and folded because her life depended on it. When the story came out in the newspapers about a young girl on her deathbed who had completed 644 cranes, Japanese schoolchildren took up her project for her, furiously racing to save her life. She died before the thousandth crane was completed.

Danny will not reveal his wish, he tells me, until he can clarify one sticky detail. I imagine that the detail is whether the telling annihilates the wish. Like a birthday wish that doesn't come true because you say it out loud. Danny says he cannot recall whether he has to make his wish *before* or *after* completing the cranes. If his wish comes after, then he says he can take all the time he needs before committing to a wish. However, if he is to make his wish *before*, then he will make 999 cranes . . . and stop.

"You know me," he says, folding his arms.

Anyway, it seems he'll never have to worry about his wish because he has decided that any crane he gives away doesn't count. Any crane that he doesn't keep in his home doesn't count. Perhaps, he will decide that blue cranes don't count, and neither do cranes made before 11:00 a.m. or after 11:00 p.m. Or, that any crane that anyone else has touched or seen doesn't count. It is a cliff-hanger. Will there ever be a thousandth crane—or a single stork—in his life?

I have a 999-crane marriage. Me, a marriage counselor who has spent the best of my years believing that any marriage can work if the couple wants it to work. No matter how much psychotherapy I studied, how many hours I spent in the library, how many other marriages I witnessed and commented on, it seemed I did not know enough yet to fix my own marriage. So after graduation I continued my studies for two years at an institute for family therapy. I was the one taking copious notes in the first row. I was the one sending away for sixty-two audiotapes of marriage counselors doing live demonstrations. When I attended a conference, I never went to the hotel pool instead of the lectures. I even went to the 7:00 a.m. breakfast meetings where we spent hours watching videotapes of famous psychotherapists' cases.

What a joke! I save marriages, but I can't save mine.

The condor is no longer on the endangered species list, but my marriage is. In all these years we'd never discussed nesting habits—the small and mighty things I would insist my own flock discuss before getting married. I never asked him: Do you want children? Do you pay your credit card bills on time? Can we divvy up the housework? I never asked him: Would you ever move out of New York City? Can we go to my parents for Thanksgiving? Will you tell me how much debt you have? I never asked him: Can we decorate our apartment? Can we throw a big party? Can we get a dog?

It must have taken incredible thought for me not to think of asking. Although it's true that if people discussed all the major marriage issues in advance, *no one* would *ever* get married.

Why is Danny's girl so far away? And for so long? Why isn't she in his arms? Why am I married? Should Danny and I trade seats? Can he help me at this point more than I can help him?

Once, during another one of our therapeutic incarnations, many years ago, Danny and I did change seats. He visited me back then because, as a child, he was bullied. He could not forget the bullies, and he seemed to find them again and again. A much younger therapist then, I asked too many questions because silence scared me. Slyly, he suggested we change seats. He had a few questions of his own. I took his seat and found terror there. A sea turtle stepped on my lungs, and I knew what it felt like to be Danny. He was being bullied, and I was bullying. Did he turn me into the bully? Or did he find me because I was a bully? Was I accommodating *his* character or was he accommodating *mine*? What about the seven-thousand-mile distance I experienced with a husband who was sitting ten feet away from me? Was I accommodating *his* character or was he accommodating *mine*?

Maybe I never asked the right questions because I was too busy writing books about relationships to have one of my own. I was too busy shopping for something to wear on *Oprah*, too busy going on *Oprah*, too busy calling everyone to tell them I was going on *Oprah*, and too busy calling everyone to ask them how I did on *Oprah*. I went off to Houston, to Seattle, to Minneapolis, to Orlando, to Boston, to teach seminars about relationships and sell books. At one point I was teaching sixty seminars a year. The rest of the time I spent getting interviewed by *Cosmopolitan* and CNN, giving the media hour-long interviews about how to keep your lover for life. Where was my husband while I spent all this time helping others? What was it like for him to have me for a wife?

On my first visit to the *Today* show, I was beside myself with excitement when they told me that Bryant Gumbel was going to interview me. Two minutes later I was beside myself with anxiety when they went on to explain that he wasn't nice to women who talked about relationships. He felt such segments were beneath him. Nervous and sleep-deprived, I had gotten up at 4:30 that morning. I was in the studio at 5:30 a.m., in full makeup at 6:00 a.m., sitting with Bryant Gumbel at 7:00 a.m., standing up to him at 7:03 when he tried to get my goat, shrinking from him at 7:04 when he had a better comeback, smiling at him at

7:05 when he softened the tiniest bit, and off the show at 7:06. At 7:30 a.m. I was standing at my apartment door again, my workday over. I wanted to scream to the world, "I survived being Gumbeled!"

When I entered our apartment, flushed and excited, heavily made up, my husband was standing there with a toilet brush and a can of Comet that he promptly handed to me.

I laughed and laughed and laughed. My husband was a riot. At 7:05 a.m. I had been with Bryant Gumbel in front of millions. At 8:05 a.m. I would be cleaning the toilet.

Was that funny?

Do I have a habit of making *everything* funny in order to survive? Am I too scared to stop laughing? When I make my patients laugh, am I offering a perceptual shift or am I diverting them from painful feelings—feelings *I* don't want to have?

Eventually, Danny stopped folding animals and started writing Italian sonnets on his old blue jeans. He went on to writing precise haiku, pages and pages of it. Meanwhile, I decided to write another book so I could save my marriage. How could I save Danny if I couldn't save myself? But how could I save my marriage if my husband wouldn't read my books? Maybe my books were too long. Maybe Danny understood that thought—maybe that's why he went from Italian sonnets to haiku.

So many times I begged my husband to read a chapter because he was so smart that the smallest thing he said was usually brilliant. I would hand him five pages and go sit in the other room so as not to annoy him. For five minutes, twenty minutes, ninety minutes, I'd sit and watch the clock. When he never came to get me, I would walk out to find him sleeping with the first page still in his hand. Why did my books put him to sleep? Why could he never, ever, ever read a page I wrote? Why did I so desperately believe that he was the only one who could help me? Why did I so desperately require him to disappoint me that I'd make him do it over and over again?

When I asked him, or more to the point, pleaded with him—when I wept and nagged—he'd tell me, "I don't know anything about books. Do you want me to check your punctuation and spelling? That I can do."

"But you know if you like something," I'd counter. "You know me," I'd tack on.

Following the advice from my marriage counseling book, I'd try asking him at different times of the day, different days of the week, in different tones of voice—even in different outfits. I wanted him to show some enthusiasm for my life. Maybe it was just that my timing was off.

If he would not read my books, I decided to see if he would listen to my music. I bought a heartbreak CD—Bill Frisell playing the music of Elvis Costello and Burt Bacharach. "Now I have nothing so God give me strength"—I played that song over and over, until my husband passed by me. I waved my hand and called out, "This is my heartbreak record." He waved back. So I took off my wedding ring in front of him and said, "Maybe I have arthritis. This hurts my finger." He said, "Oh." My husband did not see me fading. He did not know he could put his hand right through me and touch the wall.

DANNY AND I are waiting. How long should we wait?

I REMEMBER, YEARS ago, when I returned home from my first book tour, my husband had strung streamers covered with stickers of adorable cartoon ducks and hearts all across the same entrance where he handed me the toilet brush after the *Today* show.

"These are love ducks," he told me with a grand gesture toward the yellow, furry ones. "When I was a kid, I had a friend named Hugh Churchill. He died a few years ago," he said sadly. "Hugh had two baby ducklings in his backyard. They sat all day with their heads leaning on each other, snuggling, totally at peace, totally happy. But when you moved them away from each other, even a few inches away, they would quack desperately and spin in aimless circles. Even from a few inches, they couldn't find each other. It was a pitiful sound they made. Then, we'd put them back together and the very second they found each other, they leaned their heads on each other, and they stopped quacking. They were the love ducks, and now we're the love ducks. We're lost without each other."

We happily quacked and turned in circles.

I decided to keep trying.

One day Danny told me he had met a new woman at work who wrote haiku, too. She swam, she had long fingers, she listened to the Cowboy Junkies and Coltrane, *and* she said that her best first date would be spent in Home Depot.

The following week he came back flushed and folding. He said that his desk at work was a crane asylum. His kitchen was a crane lodge. His bedroom was a crane sanctuary. His sink was a birdbath. He was at 849 and counting. He dreamed he was flying over the ocean, only to land in his office cafeteria with a pint of fried rice and two pairs of chopsticks and a girl who could hammer a nail and whistle a tune.

His wish was to make love to her. He said with certainty that if he made love to her once, she would be his forever. Then he left my office.

I squeezed my eyes shut, and wished: *I wish . . . I wish my . . . I wish my husband . . . I-wish-my-husband-would-move-out-and-take-ALL-of-his-stuff-with-him. I wish to live alone in my house with my two dogs, my Brazilian Portuguese CDs, my goldfish placemats, my big bathtub, my shriveling estrogen count, my white sage and sweetgrass. I wish that my husband's family would forget my phone number and never ask me what happened. I wish for someone else to tell my patients, and I wish to receive only empathy and kindness from them. I wish I were an ex-wife by tomorrow morning.*

Suddenly, I began to whoop and holler and dance on one leg. My eyes turned red, and my head shrank. My arms flattened against my sides and I let out a wild and startling hoot. My feathers were flying everywhere.

. . .

why I stayed married: reason #1

MY GREAT AUNT Irene called from Phoenix to tell me she was diagnosed with ovarian cancer and that Lil, her partner of forty-eight years, was pissing in their bed. Alzheimer's. Aunt Irene wanted me to visit her while she could still take me out to Denny's for a Grand Slam breakfast.

It was August. You could toast wieners on the sidewalk. Arizona's claim of no humidity did little to recommend it. My husband came with me.

The Grand Slam breakfast was never to be. My aunt was rushed to the hospital clutching her stomach and screaming in pain. Hours later, the right morphine cocktail blended into my aunt like that first dribble of cream into coffee.

In and out she drifted peacefully that day while we sat in the hospital singing "Beautiful Dreamer" to her beloved Lil, who remembered the words to the song yet did not seem to know my aunt's name. While she slept we ran to her house to find her favorite beaded mukluks and brought them to her. We grabbed her tape recorder so she could listen to the Andrews Sisters sing "Don't Sit Under the Apple Tree."

As we waited for her to wake up, I told my husband the story of how, when stationed as a Wac in Hawaii during

World War II, Irene first saw Lil. Lil was married, but they discovered they both came from the same town, and soon they were inseparable. After the war ended, they both returned to Springfield, Massachusetts, resuming their separate lives. Lil went back to her husband. Aunt Irene moved into her sister's (my grandmother's) house, the same house she'd grown up in and the same house I grew up in years later. She slept in a tiny room at the foot of the attic, took correspondence courses in writing, and developed the habit of slicking her short, wavy hair straight back with a huge dab of Alberto VO5 from a tube. She called it "slickum," and she totally ignored the fact that the commercials all said, "A little dab'll do ya."

One afternoon in 1947 my aunt went to the corner pharmacy to pick up a tube of the VO5. She bumped into Lil, who told her that her husband had recently died of stomach cancer, and she was moving to Arizona to start over. In fact, the packed car was right outside, and she'd just stopped to fill a prescription before taking off. Lil said she didn't know anyone in Arizona, and that's why she chose it.

My aunt said, "You can't make a trip like that alone." She ran home, stuffed her old army duffel bag with her lumberjack shirts, her slickum, and her short stories, hopped into Lil's coupe, and left for Arizona that very hour. They'd been together ever since, Lil working forty years at the supermarket checkout counter in her white cowboy boots, Irene at Ma Bell, showing up every day with a patent-leather head.

Just then, my aunt woke up, sleepily winked at my chubby husband with his big hands and sad eyes, and said, "You look like my dad. He had the same face and the same big belly. He used to pull me into his lap, and he let me rest my head on it." Then, she added, "Can I rest my head on your belly, daddy?"

My husband took off his shoes, delicately negotiating the jungle of tube and wire as he climbed into bed next to her. She curled her arms around his legs, smiling sweetly. He rubbed her hairless head.

"You're my good, good girl," he whispered again and again until she fell asleep.

chapter 2

She's Not Very Professional, Is She, Mother?

*L*ong before I met Danny, long before I was an author of self-help books, long before I'd even had a thought of going to social work school, I was sitting in a Boston bar with my friend Donna, listening to a trio. We both noticed the bass player. "He's a cutie. I'm talking altar," Donna said. There he stood on the bandstand with the bass angled against his crotch, wearing a tuxedo, a red bow tie, and a great smile. In most bands, drummers and bass players, the two guys who hooked up the tempos, communicated with each other exclusively. But this bass player was paying attention to the audience. Donna and I felt deeply connected to him. I decided to buy a round of drinks for the band, ensuring that we'd all end up talking after the set.

He had the most distinctive voice I'd ever heard. It was croaky huckleberry, soft and briary and very sexy. Everything he said sounded seductive. I was always sensitive to voices—tones and twangs and registers—and his hit my complex chord. And the jazz? It added the touch of mystery that made him irresistible to me.

At that time I had a part-time job in a dating service, fixing people up and teaching them strategies for how to be more charming. I used each one of those strategies—eye contact, the three-second gentle wrist touch, the leaning forward breast brush—all the tricks destined to be published in the book I'd one day write called *Fifty Ways to Find a Lover*.

When the guys went back to the bandstand, Donna and I had our first fight. We both wanted him. She claimed she should have him because they both drank beer. I claimed I should have him because I had paid for the beer. Gracious Donna gave in, and, at the end of the night, he and I made plans to meet at a health food restaurant for lunch.

Since he was a musician, I decided, as I sat waiting in front of the health food restaurant, that I should expect to pay my way. Ten minutes later I was tapping my foot, still waiting. He was late—twenty minutes in all when he finally rattled up in a VW bus that hadn't seen a good day since the sixties. It smoked, it choked, even the dents had dents.

What a shock when he got out of the car!

Where was the tuxedo?

The splashy bow tie?

He was wearing a horizontally striped polo shirt and a faint plaid pair of Bermuda shorts, white socks, and his black tuxedo shoes.

We sat awkwardly in the restaurant, I think because I kept expecting him to apologize for what he was wearing. Eventually we began to talk about music. He impressed me with his knowledge of jazz, although he could have impressed me by reading the telephone book with that great voice. I found out that he'd recently returned from a tour in Japan and would soon leave for a tour of Europe. I knew the names of musicians he worked with from my record collection. He'd played on albums, too. He lived in New York City.

The mismatched clothing faded away.

As we perused the menu, he said, "I've eaten here before. Whatever you order, you ought to try the bread basket, too. It's great here."

Deciding to hint that I was paying for my lunch, I said, "Ummm, I think I'm going to order a sandwich, so I'm already having bread. Besides, the bread basket is four dollars. I'd rather just pay for the sandwich."

He replied, "Don't worry about the money."

Now I don't know what *you* think when someone says not to worry about the money, but I assumed he was treating me.

Imagine my surprise when the bill came and he said, "I

owe six dollars for my sandwich, and you owe six dollars for your sandwich and four dollars for the bread basket."

We paid and walked outside, where I watched him use a screwdriver to open the broken driver's seat door and lift himself in. My last glimpse was of a white athletic sock in a black dress shoe.

I vowed never to go out with him again. That would have been that if he had asked me out in the next month. He didn't.

One night he offered me a free pass to see Gladys Knight & The Pips because he was playing in the band. After the concert, he invited me backstage while he played a few hands of poker with the other musicians—just enough to pay for the drinks we ordered in a late-night jazz club. He introduced me to all the musicians. I felt honored that he wanted them to see us together. I never gave a second thought to the fact that he spent more than an hour gambling on our second date.

After a cognac or two, I got up the nerve to ask about our last date. He explained that his previous girlfriend was a radical feminist who blew up if he reached for the check. He said he got so nervous, he didn't know what to do.

I understood completely.

I let the question about the stripes and plaids go.

Then, as if the second date was not perfect enough, he sent flowers to the dating service where I worked with a card that read, "I'm looking for an exciting, mysterious woman for a late-night rendezvous. Can you help?"

Part of why we hit it off so well was that I was in the music business, too. I'd been working as a singer for more than ten years. The dating service job was something I did part-time for extra income and fun.

As a vocalist, I'd done every kind of gig there was, from being a singing waitress to entertaining at roadhouses to opening for B.B. King, Little River Band, and Victor Borge. Once, I arrived at a job to discover that I was singing in a strip club, and I was the only woman in the place wearing clothes. Another time, I jammed backstage with Taj Mahal, who invited me to sing with him after I told him that I'd gone to school with his sister, Connie. Singing with wedding bands, I'd consumed more than five thousand pieces of wedding cake. Eventually, I could tell in glance whether the bride and groom had a prayer of living up to their "I do's." But sometimes, I had more information than a glance—more information than I wanted. Like the night the band was on break and we entered a stairwell to drink the shots we had sneaked with the help of the bartender. There, one flight down in a corner, we could see the bride humping the caterer. She was too drunk to care that we were there.

While I was dating the bass player, my life started changing. My friend Tony and I invented an adult education class called *Fifty Ways to Find a Lover*. After the first class, I continued developing and teaching it myself. My friend Ross talked me into writing the book based on the class. I received twenty-six rejection letters from twenty-six editors who remarked that I had no credentials, although the well-known editor, Nan Talese, wife of author Gay Talese, wrote, "The author is very pretty."

After nine months I sold the book, and then made the purely economic decision to apply to Hunter College School of Social Work in order to get credentials.

At least, I'd have sworn to that until the day I was accepted, when I broke down in tears and cried for a whole week. Only then did I realize that I applied to social work school because I wanted to feel better, and nothing else had worked to kill off the mass of pain inside me.

Enclosed in an emotional safe, the pain was lodged somewhere deep inside me, but I could not locate its position. I had a kidney removed, my tonsils, my appendix— but I didn't get any closer to finding it. Always there, it didn't shift, it didn't move, it didn't give. It was kind of like a breast implant, but a pain implant instead, filled with all the things that ever hurt me.

There were so many times during my life when, just like when I broke my wrist roller-skating, I could not ask for help. I couldn't understand any of them, and I couldn't seem to do any better when a new situation arose.

One morning as I was entering my seventh-grade homeroom, someone pushed me into a wall. A freshly sharpened pencil went through the fake leather of my pocketbook, through my skirt, and broke off flush in my thigh. Shocked, I looked in my pocketbook to discover that a good inch of the pencil was missing.

From 8:30 a.m. to 3:00 p.m., I attended classes with a pencil in my leg. I told no one. I never sought out the nurse. Again, I walked home from school, and I waited until dinnertime to tell my parents what had happened to me.

I know this is not what children do when they get hurt.

Years later, in my thirties, I was in a club dancing with a friend when I fell. The bone in my left arm popped through my skin. Instead of telling my friend, I threw a jacket over it and drove myself to a hospital. The doctor and nurses doped me up, set the compound fracture, and told me someone had to pick me up. I drove myself home.

I know this is not what adults do when they get hurt.

So you see why, at age thirty-eight, my call to social work school was urgent.

Twenty years of being a patient in psychotherapy had made me more socially acceptable. Twenty years of being a patient in psychotherapy had made people like me better. Twenty years of being a patient in psychotherapy had made me function better.

I just wasn't *feeling* better, and I thought if I could learn how to help other people treat themselves better, this knowledge might also end up helping me.

I WAS ENGAGED to the bass player when my first book was published. One day, I received a call from Sun Features for an interview about flirting. I never asked what Sun Features was, and, to this day, I don't know if it exists.

The article came out several weeks later in a very popular issue of the *National Enquirer* with a blowsy Ted Kennedy on the cover.

That same morning, my phone rang, and on the other end was . . . *The Oprah Winfrey Show*. They were doing a show on good pick-up lines, and, having seen the article, they were interested in adding me to the panel. Pick-up lines, both good and bad, were my well-researched specialty of the moment because I had begun writing a chapter about them. I was on a pick-up line roll.

"Your feet must be very tired, because you've been walking through my mind all day."

"Wanna come back to my place and break a few commandments?"

"Can I buy you a drink or would you rather just have the money?"

After hearing my stories, *Oprah* called me back and told me they'd dumped all the other panel guests. The producer said, "You're the *only* guest. Do you understand? You aren't *on* the show. You *are* the show, and you'd better be great. Now, get a good night's rest."

A good night's rest? I begged my husband to pretend he was Oprah. He interviewed me over and over and over again.

As they escorted me onto the stage and sat me there—alone—my knees were knocking, my heart was pounding. I had never been so thirsty in my life. Then, they left me alone for fifty minutes . . . with Oprah . . . and thirteen million other people.

In a blink, it was over.

Oprah came over to me and looked me up and down, as if close up I appeared different. Then she said she loved my dress, *and* she loved my hair, *and* she loved my earrings, *and* she loved my attitude. She invited me back soon.

My publicists immediately demanded raises.

In the end, I was to appear on *Oprah* eight times, but on that first day, dazed, I rode to O'Hare in a white limousine wondering what kind of impact this might have on my identity as a social worker. Would I still be taken seriously? Waiting for my flight, I called my friend Ross, who told me my choices: "Do you want to be a social worker or a star?"

I waited the two weeks for my episode of *Oprah* to air.

I thought about my secret double life as a flirting instructor and the embarrassment it caused me in social work school. There I sat with the gifted therapy scholar whose last book sold sixty copies. She would never go on *Oprah* because she wore knee-highs. She didn't know that fashion counted on television at least as much as the message.

I didn't want her to know that, in addition to writing papers about Dominican immigration, I was writing books about flirting.

Welfare policy, community organizing, borderline personality disorders, schizophrenia, a workshop called *72 Ways to Flirt*—what didn't fit? I remember when one classmate said to me, "I work with battered wives. I wish I could do something light like what you do." I wanted to scream,

"Loneliness isn't light! The people who take flirting classes are miserable!"

With a week to wait until the episode aired, I couldn't sleep. I tossed and turned on an emotional bandstand with a full diagnostical rhythm section. I thought about how I'd left the narcissistic music business only to discover that psychotherapy has as many prima donnas, honkers who love to hear themselves honk. I realized that therapists love the audience as much as any saxophone player does.

Was I describing myself? I felt embarrassed and ridiculous, and yet, I wanted to be a star anyway.

A day to wait.

And then it happened.

One day I was a grad student writing a thesis on black women's working conditions during the period between 1880 and 1910, and the next day the woman behind the deli counter across the street screamed, "I saw you on *O-O-Oprah!*" She promptly named a deli sandwich after me.

Could it be any clearer? I would not work nine to nine in an agency. What if I got a call to go on television on a workday? I couldn't be asking a boss for permission not to have my session with a recent rape victim because I had to take an afternoon off to be on *Entertainment Tonight*.

Yet I had no right to consider going into private practice so soon. Wouldn't I be universally hated by social workers who were earning eighteen thousand dollars a year for sixteen-hour days in underfunded halfway houses?

This dilemma was preempted by another. Having

established myself in front of thirteen million viewers as an expert in relationships, it occurred to me that it might be time to try to get my first patient.

I ANSWERED AN ad in the paper and sublet an office two days a week from Dr.-Takes-out-Chinese-food-and-leaves-the-smelly-cartons-in-the-wastebasket-overnight. Little did I know that my work would suffer not only from inexperience, but at least as much from the overpowering stench of old moo goo gai pan.

Weeks passed. Where were my patients? I had an office, but I had no sense of how to get anyone into it. I belonged to no professional organizations except the musicians' union. I had no source of referrals. While there were many other offices on my floor, I never thought of introducing myself to my neighbors and giving them my business card, or of sending out announcements that said I was expanding my practice—as in, say, from nobody to anybody.

Finally, I decided to do something I knew how to do. Based on the flirting and dating workshops I'd been teaching for five years, I decided to start a group for people who wanted to get more dates. I placed an ad in the personals section of *New York* magazine. The ad said that I, the author of *Guerrilla Dating Tactics*, was forming a six-session group to teach dating techniques to the clamoring public at large. At the top of the ad was the publicist's mantra: "As seen on *Oprah*." On the bottom of the ad, it said, "limited space," which sounded as if the group was nearly full, but really meant that I could only fit six people in my office at one time.

My phone, which had not rung at all before, suddenly rang all day. One caller asked, "Do you think you can help me find a girlfriend to take to my cousin's wedding in two weeks? I come from a big Italian family, and if I show up alone again, my Uncle Vinny is gonna tell everyone I'm gay."

Another caller asked, "Would I have to come to the group every week, and if I don't come, do I have to pay? Because it isn't fair that you ask me to pay for a group I'm not in."

Yet another asked, "What are the ages and weights of the women who will be in the group?"

And yet another asked, "Where did you get your under-graduate and your graduate degrees, and in what years? Also, can you give me a list of your references—you know, satisfied clients who have been through your training and gotten married?" The most common call I got was, "Can I try it out for a week to see if I like it?"

The strangest call I got was, "I'd like to come to the group, but I'd have to do it on speaker phone because I'm a very high-profile person, and I don't want to be recognized."

Several of the people who called asked if they could come see me alone. Even though this is what I wanted, it amazed me—this picking a therapist from a magazine ad.

Two days later, my phone stopped ringing.

My sound bite was over.

Finally, I got it.

Having seen me on television didn't necessarily mean they wanted me for their therapist. All they really wanted was to know more about Oprah.

What's she really like?

Who does her hair?

MY VERY FIRST patient was Sinclair (a family name dating back to the Mayflower), a middle-aged man with thin, brown hair on a fair, thin-skinned scalp. In the movies he would be played by the love child of a maniacal Christopher Walken and a rumpled yet jolly Tom Ewell.

In the style of therapy I studied in social work school, the first step, after finding out the problem, was to take a detailed family history, going back as far as possible. For example, who came over on the Mayflower, who survived the first year in Plymouth, and who was depressed? But the first step in the style of therapy I was currently reading about from my psychotherapy book club was to find out the problem and then ask the miracle question: "If I could wave a magic wand and make a miracle, what would you be doing that you aren't doing now?"

When I asked Sinclair to tell me about his family history, he wrinkled his nose like he suddenly smelled the bad Chinese food and said, "Tell me how to pick up women at the Polo Lounge. I already know my family history. Give me something I can use."

Aha, I thought, he's a miracle question patient. So I said, "If I could perform a miracle—"

Sinclair interrupted me and asked, "How much do you charge?" Before I gleaned that I could have doubled my fee, he said, "I'm coming twice a week. Mondays and Thursdays will work. Mondays and Fridays are better. That way, I can debrief on Mondays and get a pep talk on Fridays."

Thus, Sinclair entered my office twice a week, completing multiple sentences before he approached the couch. The Polo Lounge, Bemelman's at The Carlyle, the bar at the "21" Club, Four Seasons—Sinclair wanted coaching in his preferred technique of sidling up to women and inserting himself into their conversations.

"First I scope the room. When I see a group of women talking, I walk over and stand next to them until they get used to me being there. Then, if they don't change tables, I ask a question like, 'Have you lovely ladies been here long?' I hand my business card to whoever answers me. Then, I invite her to lunch at Le Cirque. Lunch is a good first date. If she seems nervous, I explain that the maître d' knows me."

As Sinclair made his rounds of the who's who of bars in New York City, I tried to convince my husband to buzz my waiting room while Sinclair was in session. "Please, please, please. It looks so bad if I only have one patient, if no one ever buzzes while he's there."

My husband agreed and disagreed. "I'll buzz the waiting room, but I'm not coming in. I'll drive you home, but you can't talk about work in the car." I was generally revved up when I left my office—having only one patient and all— and he found my excited chatter about therapy annoying. If I persisted, he used a variety of tactics to shut me up. For example, he might start talking about computer languages and ask my opinion. Or worse, he would talk about ethics: "Do you really think it's *ethical* to discuss your patient with me? Aren't there rules about that?" In the end, we would ride home, he in silence, I in shame.

Why was it like that? This is a question I never asked then, but I can answer it now:

My husband did not want to pick me up at work, but he couldn't say that.

He did not want to make my life easier because I didn't make his life easier.

Picking me up at work meant he would have to come home from his day job and spend time with me.

He didn't want to spend time with me because he hated his day job, and it was my fault he had one.

The reason it was my fault was that, when we were dating, he was always broke. I got relationship advice from a friend who told me to say, "If you want to fuck me from behind while I'm wearing black high heels you better be able to take me out to dinner and pay for it."

So he took a day job and, while he said he hated it, he was seduced by his IRA, pension, health insurance, and misery. He was seduced by his own misery, which he could use to blame me.

He'd pick me up.

I'd have to pay.

With the two of us, a fifty-block car ride home could get that complicated.

I WANTED TO talk about work more than anything else. I wanted to try to understand so many things, like why Sinclair would refuse to tell me his family history. What was the big deal? That got me thinking. Why would I be curious about Sinclair's family history as a way to understand him when I actually married a man without giving a second thought to *his* family history? What about my own family history? How is it that my mother and stepfather still hadn't met my husband's parents, even after we'd been together for ten years—even though they all lived in the same state? How had I never thought about that, or done anything about it? How was it my husband never mentioned it either? Did we have some kind of conspiracy? If we did, why?

DURING OUR FOURTH session, Sinclair entered the room whining that things weren't moving fast enough. Pointing a finger at me, he said, "I'm still hearing a lot more noes than yeses. You're keeping something back, something important. Will you tell me if I come three times a week?" He added, "You call yourself an expert. You *are* an expert, aren't you?"

What I thought was: *How would you know? You never listen to anything I say. You're talking when you walk into the waiting room, talking the whole time in my office, refusing to answer any questions that I think are relevant.*

I considered Sinclair's rumpled jacket, the pocket stuffed with a snotty, maroon handkerchief, the buttons pulling from the effort of his midriff to bypass them, and his pale, shiny head appearing in horizontal stripes beneath his pale, shiny hair. Then I considered my financial and emotional need to be the expert Sinclair wanted me to be.

I concluded that he'd have to become charming.

Using "miracle techniques" based on the miracle question, I took a new tack: I became Sinclair's Vince Lombardi, his Knute Rockne, his Pat Riley. I explained that rather than challenging women so early on, he might want to learn more about building rapport. I suggested things to say and things not to say. His propensity to mention his unusual rashes and coo over his alma mater, for example, might not be appealing to women in their forties. I pointed him toward the door and told him to go get 'em.

The following week, Sinclair entered my office and paced the room, turning toward me and pointing his lengthy, pale finger.

"You're wrong," he said gleefully. "I met Stella. We have everything in common—including the psoriasis," he added triumphantly. Sinclair told me that they had a tennis date the following day, and that weekend they were going to play golf at Stella's country club.

Miracle question therapy was working.

Being a therapist was so fulfilling.

Sinclair was improving.

I planned my next ad.

The next week, Sinclair fired me. Stella wasn't who he thought she was and neither was I. Stella had cellulite in her tennis shorts. I talked too much. He didn't like the country club she belonged to. He didn't like my cheap shoes. She wasn't as good a golfer as she had led him to believe. I wasn't as good a therapist.

As he sat there telling me how I had let him down, I wanted to scream: *You're disappointed in me? What about me? You made me an expert in your head and that expert has nothing to do with who I am. You never listened to me. I was never a real person to you. You have no idea who I am!*

When my husband picked me up that night, I was going to let him have it: *What about me? I want to talk about my psychotherapy work, the most important thing to me. You've made me a wife in your head, and that wife has nothing to do with who I am. You never listen to me. I'm not a real person to you!*

Sinclair finished writing me a final check. He rose and walked to the door. With his hand on the knob, he remarked that I reminded him of his sister, who had committed suicide when he was seventeen, and that Stella had taken the same medicine as his aunt, who had been institutionalized. Also, had he forgotten to mention that he already had several other therapists, and he liked all of them better than me? He walked out of my office snickering to himself, "She's not very professional, is she, mother?"

With tears in my eyes I ran down to the car, where my irritated husband was waiting to pick me up. I tried to tell him about Sinclair, but he coldly said I had to choose: either he'd listen to me, or we could go to 23rd and Park to pick up two Tasti D-Lite cones—one with sprinkles, one with nuts.

I went for the food.

It was late, and having my only patient fire me made me hungry.

•   •   •

why I stayed married: **reason #2**

MY HUSBAND IS not just any bass player; he is a gifted bass player. He's played concerts all over the world, and he's recorded a number of CDs. He even played on a couple of Spike Lee movie soundtracks. Yet, no matter how important the gig, he's always waited until the last possible minute to shower and get dressed to go. He left no time for the inevitable catastrophe. Some nights he would call out, "I can't find my bass wheel. Did you see it?" Other nights he'd say, "I wore my bow tie last night, but I can't find it. Did you move it?" Or, "I can only find one of my cuff links. Do you have a paper clip?" Or, "Did you see my suspenders?" Or, "Where's my music?"

These nuisances, these objects that eluded him, were all thrown carelessly at the end of the last gig in looming piles of clothes, scattered like little sphinxes across the room. We'd sack the house, throwing things right and left, only to go through the same routine all over again the following night.

On one particular night, it was a shoe, and he seemed more perplexed and anxious than ever. He grew so frantic about the shoe that he started to hyperventilate. I had to sit him down and search for it alone. I couldn't understand how one shoe could elicit so much more emotion than a bow tie or a bass wheel. Later that night, when he came home, he told me the story.

"I got invited to my first birthday party when I was five by a kid in my kindergarten class. I was so excited about it. My mother gave me a dollar to pick out a toy for him, and I shopped and shopped. It was so hard to decide. I was worried I'd pick the wrong thing. It was the first time I ever bought a present for someone else. One of the other kid's mothers was going to drive four kids, including me. I'd never gone anywhere without my family so I was excited about that, too. I guess I knew even then that other kids had parties that I wasn't invited to. A lot of the time I got left out.

"I've been running late all my life. The day of the party was no exception. I started getting ready at the last minute, and I couldn't find one of my shoes. My mother told me that if I could not find my shoe, I could not go to the party. After frantically searching for a few minutes, I gave up. I don't know how much time passed before the car pulled into the driveway. I could see the kids in the back seat. My mother motioned the car to drive on—without me."

Now I knew why the missing shoe paralyzed him. Now I knew about those mornings when I would find him sitting on the bed, holding his foot, staring off into space. I used to tease him about that. How could he stare off into space for so long? Now I knew.

He was distracted by a car filled with laughing boys.

They were jumping up and down.

Waving.

Driving off without him.

chapter 3

My First Two Marriages, or
Gimme Thirty Quarter Pounders

y second patient, Morris, was thirty-five, had graduated law school at the bottom of his class, and had no people skills or social conscience. Thus, he took a state job and became a family court lawyer. He laughed as he told me, "You know, I can't tell one family from the other because I never look at their faces anymore. I'm so bored. I make it a game to try to represent them without looking at their faces."

He angrily told me that everyone he worked with got promoted above him, disliked him, and went to lunch without him. He added that he hardly made any money and was paying only six hundred dollars a month for rent now, but would soon have to move into a bad neighborhood to lower his rent to four hundred dollars a month, because that was all he could afford. "My mom helps me out when I ask her. She has a pension. But she's cheap because my sister has metastatic cancer. She holds back money for her. My sister always got more—even before she was sick."

Yikes.

I hadn't thought about patients like Morris.

I remember my social work internship at the Jewish Guild for the Blind. One of the members in my group, a fifty-year-old man, said, "I been blind from birth. Before the guild I was pretty much on my own. Last year, they took us upstate to a petting zoo. I pet a dog before and a cat, but nothing else. And, the thing that was . . . *yow!* . . . when they handed me a bird. The bird was so loud and noisy I thought that it have a head as big as ours. Thas what I 'spected when I was gonna hold the bird. So when they hand it to me and I feel this little head, I say, 'You made a mistake. You was supposed to give me a bird.' And they say, 'This is a bird.' And then my friend who's next to me reaches over and says, 'Yeah, thas a bird. Whaddya, blind or somethin'?' And we all fall down laughing."

Then there was the day that ninety-seven-year-old Susie, blind and depressed, took my fingers with her withered hands when I asked her, "Susie, is there anything you still enjoy?" She said, as if it were a secret, "Everyone I love is dead. Everyone I know is dead. All my friends are dead."

And Rosa. I met Rosa when I was an intern at Lehman

College. She was the first in her family to attend college. "In El Salvador," Rosa reported, "when I was growing up, you never knew who was going to come home from school. They would round up the boys. Two of my brothers disappeared on the same day. A neighbor came running to the house because her son was taken. My brothers weren't home yet and my father told us all to get in the house. We never saw them again."

Sitting here with Morris, I was beginning to understand more about how therapists earn their fee in private practice.

I FELT COMPLETELY unskilled, and I came home after work in a funk. How was I supposed to help a patient I couldn't get myself to like, even a little? Worse, not being able to like Morris made it hard for me to like myself. I felt that other therapists with more talent and experience wouldn't be going through this. I waited for my husband to come home from his gig, and then I announced, "I can't help my patients because I have no talent and no experience. I hate myself."

He responded, "I lost my bass wheel."

HUNKERING DOWN THE next week, I attempted to protect Morris's ego, and I used object relations techniques to try to raise his awareness about how other people might feel (while using empathy techniques on myself so I could tolerate how *Morris* might feel). I told him I wanted to help him explore more satisfying and responsible ways to get his own needs met. Morris retorted that all he wanted was a girlfriend, and that's why he was coming to see me.

Taking a deep, slow yoga breath, I decided to take a girlfriend history, a retrospective of his historical dating habits. Had he ever had a girlfriend? What methods had he used to try to get a girlfriend in the past?

I SHIVER TO think of my own romantic past. In addition to the usual flotsam and jetsam (including the alcoholic who had me so scared that I started sleeping with my car keys in my pocket, in case I had to get away in the middle of the night), I've been married three times. Well, technically, I've been married four times, because I divorced and remarried husband number two. When I hear about people who do this, I wonder who they are, even though I'm one of them. I can tell you I was no Natalie Wood and he was no Robert Wagner.

My first two marriages, if you can call them that, were short. I married my first husband when I was nineteen. Soon after I met him, a doctor put me on eighty milligrams of Librium a day for an anxiety disorder, which I now believe was possibly created and at the least exacerbated by planning to marry someone I didn't love. He was a five-foot-six, 215-pound weight lifter who spent an inordinate amount of time measuring his nineteen-inch biceps and taking steroids even though they made his balls shrink. Sitting on the bed, he'd spread his legs and examine himself in the mirror. "They haven't shrunk that much, have they?"

I remember those strange looks at McDonald's when he'd walk up to the counter and order: "Gimme thirty Quarter Pounders." Next, he'd remove and discard the thirty buns and scarf down the beef patties, followed by a fifty-vitamin chaser. This man could clear a McDonald's faster than mad cow disease, as grossed out patrons gathered their children and their children's Happy Meals and hustled off to eat in their cars.

He was from a wealthy family who complained about their maid in her presence. "Thelma," his mother would call out, if we were eating and ran out of mayonnaise. "Thelma!" she would yell as Thelma climbed the narrow staircase up from the basement. "Thelmaaaaaaaaa!" As Thelma was replacing the empty mayonnaise jar, the mother would say, "I don't know what takes her so long. She sits there in the basement watching television. I think we should take the television out of her room."

A mutual friend introduced me to this husband during my first month at college. He was a jock, not my type. But he fell head over heels for me and my long, blonde hair. I wasn't used to that. I did not think it something to take lightly. On our second date, he announced, "I better call in the second team," and, cupping his hand to his mouth, he yelled, "Where's the second team?" When I asked him what that meant, he said he was losing the battle of trying not to fall in love with me. I found this curious and shocking.

That night, he took me on a trip through his childhood. We went to the beach where he had spent his summers, the football field where he had played in high school, the house he had grown up in, and, finally, his favorite deli. Here, while I ate my very first Reuben, he diagrammed our future on a place mat with half-sour pickles. "OK, the place mat is the playing field and here you are on the thirty-yard line," and he promptly placed a pickled pepper on that spot. Then, as if to cement the play, he reached into his varsity jacket and pulled out a jewelry box and whispered, "Touchdown."

"I'm going to marry you," he said. "Meanwhile, I don't want anyone else looking at you, so wear this." He then presented me with a wedding band, even though we'd only known each other for a few weeks. I put it on my finger. It felt good to belong to someone.

I belonged to someone I didn't love for four years. His addiction to powerlifting and football seemed like a smoke screen, a cover for deeper feelings that couldn't be measured in yards and Quarter Pounders. But I knew how my parents liked the idea of a daughter with an anxiety disorder having a rich husband. And although I didn't like his mother, who kept calling me his "goyish farm girl" (er . . . I was Jewish), I did like the outfits she bought me at Saks Fifth Avenue to fool her friends into believing I was a worthy catch.

Soon, she was talking about me in my presence in the same way she talked about Thelma: "Look at her eye shadow. She's goyish. She's got goyim blood. Look at that face. Can't you see her on a tractor in a field of hay?" She laughed and laughed and laughed.

I tried to make friends with Thelma, who was smart enough to keep away from me.

DURING ALL THIS, I was in therapy at the college counseling center, and, in keeping with my "don't tell" policy, I never mentioned to my therapist that I didn't love my fiancé. I did, however, tell her I'd never had an orgasm. I remember asking her how you know if you've had one. "You just know," she said, which was no help at all until years later, when I finally had one and knew exactly what she meant. Anyway, she never asked about him. She focused only on my early childhood. Since she was a grad student in the psychology department at my college, I think that was probably what she was studying that semester. While I was finding it hard to spend time with my fiancé and, even worse, his family, she was asking me if I had been breast-fed.

Sooner rather than later, the day arrived when my parents drove their battered Bonneville from Springfield, Massachusetts, to Woodmere, New York, to meet his parents. I was not ashamed of our lack of money because, as rich as his parents were, well, that's how beautiful my parents were. My blue-eyed, blonde mom was a perfect size eight and only saw the bright side of any matter, and my tall, handsome dad looked like a movie star (though he had held and lost more jobs than I could count, not to mention his little gambling problem). Their smashing good looks were not lost on my fiancé's mother, who tried to act more important than usual.

"Thelma!" she yelled even louder. "We're ready for dessert!" Then she turned to my parents and said, "She wanders off." My soon-to-be mother-in-law went to the refrigerator and brought out a large, flat plate covered with a sheet of wax paper. It looked like there were strips of bacon under the paper, I remember thinking. Then she pulled off the paper with a Siegfried & Roy flourish. There sat seven fancy gold watches. "Pick one," she said to me. "One of them is our engagement present to you."

There, in front of my parents, who would be lucky if they could pay the tolls on the way home, I picked the fanciest, gaudiest watch with the most diamonds and the biggest chunks of gold.

Days later, it hit me: the watch, the future, the thrill of being wanted by someone—well, they weren't enough to compensate for a guy who worked out until he threw up, discussed the protein content of his turds, and ate at his parents' house several nights a week. Three months before the wedding, I still hadn't been able to get myself to buy a dress. I had to call it off.

The idea of speaking up terrified me—and my terror

was exacerbated by the fact that no one had an inkling of how I felt.

The day before I was going to tell, the very day before, my handsome forty-one-year-old father dropped dead of a massive heart attack.

My fiancé was sent to my apartment to tell me.

He drove me home.

That night, I slept with my mother in their bed.

She did not want to be alone, and neither did I.

"We've been married twenty years, and we made love as much in the past year as we did in the first year," she confided.

That made a strong impression on me, since I was already shying away from sex with the muscle-bound hulk. I was going to tell her so right then, when she said, "Thank God I don't have to worry about you."

So I told her that I had lied to him about being a virgin.

"Carry it to your grave," she urged me.

In the Jewish tradition, weddings take precedence over funerals. Three months after my father died, just before my mother got hepatitis and mono at the same time and went into quarantine, as my grandparents traveled from Hartford to Queens in a car, crying, "The child is not supposed to die first, the child is not supposed to die first," as my sobbing uncle gave me away, and as I knew, knew, knew—but silently vowed never, ever, to say—that I wasn't in love, I got married.

My husband did not want to leave New York, as a honeymoon would conflict with his rigorous weight-training schedule. So we went from a banquet hall in Queens to the soon-to-be-condemned Lincoln Square Motor Inn in Manhattan, where we watched Part II of the *Mission: Impossible* television series. My husband, who was against sugar, poured the cheap champagne that the motel had left us down the toilet. He said, "I'll be watching your diet now, everything you eat. After all, that's part of my job," and he pinched a bit of extra flesh near my buttocks and smiled.

The next morning, our phone rang at 8:30 a.m. He turned to me and said, "My father wants to have breakfast with me so I'm gonna meet him around the corner. Then I'll get in a workout, and then we can grab a steak. What are you going to do?"

As I RELIVED these Kodak moments, I was pulled back into my smelly office, where Morris was still speaking.

"I had a few dates with this girl I met at a Shabbat dinner, but I can't stand looking at her. She invited me for dinner, and I went, but all I could think of was how to get away. She was ugly and her pot roast sucked. I got up and left. On the way home I went to Washington Street to get a quick BJ from a hooker."

Morris added that he was addicted to blow jobs from hookers. Once, twice, three times a week, if he could wheedle the money out of his mom.

Having learned in social work school to resist every urge to pathologize a patient, I decided to consider the adaptive aspect of Morris's behavior. After all, I'd seen *Working Girl*, starring Melanie Griffith, and other working-girl-with-heart-of-gold movies, not to mention *Lonesome Dove*. I asked Morris if he ever talked to the hookers—like, you know, made friendly conversation. He said, "Why would I talk to them? They're whores."

SOMEHOW, MY FIRST husband and I lasted four years.

My second husband would have liked me to be more of a whore. I met him when I was a twenty-four-year-old mediocre nightclub singer on a Sheraton hotel bandstand in a braless, "dangerous curves," ruby red dress, and he was a swarthy Italian saxophone player who could balance a burning Marlboro on the bell of his horn while imitating Cannonball Adderley. He gave me my first orgasm.

When did our problems begin? Well, they began when he opened his mouth to talk to me for the first time. "Didn't I see you jogging in the park when I was jogging in the park?" I, who did not even own sneakers, said, "Probably . . . it was probably me."

That night, he invited me to go with him to see a band at another club, where I was intoxicated by the smell of Scotch and cigarettes on his breath and began drinking Scotch and smoking cigarettes myself. The leader of the band, an Italian trumpet player named Doug, was famous for eating salami sandwiches, packed by his wife, that made him burp and fart on the stand all night. Doug's wife was a sly cookie—even if he'd wanted to cheat on her, no one would have him.

On the bandstand he made you stand right next to him, with that sadistic, salami-sated smile on his face. I didn't know this when my brave second husband-to-be stood next to him and blew a hundred choruses of "Song for My Father" in a Herbie Mann style on the flute.

One night, he said, "I love you," and he climbed between my legs. When he resurfaced, he added, "I'm married. But, you have to understand. I cheated on her while we were on our honeymoon. She got sunburned and wanted to take a nap, so I went down to the hotel bar. There was a woman there who started telling me that she had a little scar on her breast, and I told her I wanted to see it. The next thing I knew we were in her room looking for the scar. But there was no scar."

Later, I found out that he had two young daughters, ages three and five. He happily left his wife and children to be with me. Then he happily left me and went back to them. Then he happily left all of us for an affair with a waitress he'd met while he and I were having a romantic dinner out. Then he came back to me. He was so sorry that he would make it up by giving me oral sex for hours.

I did not give him up.

God knows we had enough problems, but our problems got worse when he got kinky, and I wasn't kinky enough. He started off with dirty books, dirty talk, dildos. Then he said, "Tell me about other men you want to do it with."

I did what he asked. I told him about other men I did it with while we did it, but that didn't hold his interest much because there weren't many other men, so I had to repeat myself a lot.

"Tell me what they looked like, tell me how they were hung, tell me how long you knew them before you fucked them, tell me what you'd do if one of them walked into the room right now. You'd like that, wouldn't you? One to fuck you and one to watch, or one for the bottom and one for the top. Tell me how much you'd like that. Maybe I'll go out right now and find one and bring him back."

One night, my prayers were answered when he proposed. I told him that I was so in love with him that I wanted to have his baby. I wanted the two of us to begin our own little family.

He promptly broke up with me again.

Weeks later, he came back with a list of names for our child.

We had a little wedding on February 27, 1977.

On May 16, 1977, the condom broke.

Soon after, I told him, "I'm pregnant. I'm throwing up."

He threw his arms around me.

He pulled me close and whispered my name over and over.

He said, "We'll have children. More than one. As many as you want. But we can't start now. I already have two kids under six. Please . . . sweetheart . . . please . . . we'll wait a few years so we can do it right."

Upon his request (which graduated quickly into a wild insistence), I made an appointment for an abortion.

When I came back to the waiting room after the procedure, he said, "I don't want it."

"We're not having it," I answered.

"No," he said, "I don't want the marriage."

"We're still getting presents," I said dumbly. "We have three toaster ovens."

He put on his jacket, and he left.

A week later, he still hadn't come back. A few days after that, I was checked into a psychiatric hospital, refusing to eat or sleep, swearing that this was all just a terrible mistake.

Thirty days passed. Therapy couldn't shake me. The psychiatric crew invited him to attend group therapy, where he sat in front of thirty-seven other patients and said, "I don't love you. I don't want to be with you. "

"Yes, you do," I replied with an easy, relaxed voice and a secret smile.

I GOT RELEASED. He came back. One night, while we were in a bar with a few friends, I went to the very crowded ladies' room. Shortly thereafter, he said to my friend, "She's been gone too long. Go in the ladies' room and look under the stalls. She's wearing boots. See if you see her boots."

My friend came in and apparently didn't look too hard because, even though I was there peeing, she came out and told him she didn't see my boots.

He didn't say a word until we got in the car to go home. Then he slammed his fist so hard against the windshield that it cracked. He said, "You're sucking off strangers in the parking lot. Get out of this car and walk home, you cunt." When I finally arrived at home, he greeted me with thirty-two ounces of V8 juice—thrown at my head—still in the thirty-two-ounce can. "You're a lying," he said slowly, "cheating," his voice rising and quivering, "cunt with a capital C." Then the V8 juice can whizzed past my head and broke the glass in the screen door.

And, yes, if you are wondering, drugs were involved.

WE BROKE UP and got back together again more times than I can count. Finally, I mustered the sense to leave town, running away with an even worse guy to get rid of this guy. Years after we split, this ex-husband tracked me down in Boston. He said he had a question for me. I thought he was going to ask about us—about what happened to us, about why we didn't work. Instead he said, "You were always so clean. Can you tell me how to ask my new girlfriend to wash her genitals before we have sex without hurting her feelings?"

MORRIS NEVER GOT near the hooker's genitals. She was not a person to him—just a warm, wet sucking. He had no empathy for her. Did he have empathy for anyone? Could he muster some for his dying sister? Morris wasn't inter-ested in his sister. He preferred to use therapy to consider tactics to get his mom to lend him more money, or, as a last resort, to find even cheaper living quarters.

And so I did my job, part of which seemed to be to hear the unspeakable come out of the mouth of the unbearable. I was able to listen, able to tolerate anything. As you can see from my marriages, I'd had practice.

At the end of our first month of therapy, I presented Morris with a bill. He said he'd pay me the following week, but the following week, he forgot his checkbook. That made five sessions at seventy-five dollars that he owed me. I told him he needed to pay me at the next session, and he said, "No problem." Should I have been surprised when, on that day, he left a message on my machine that he was quitting therapy? He told me not to call him. He stressed that he didn't want to speak to me, and said he would mail me my check. Of course, I never received the check. My bills were returned when Morris moved again to an even cheaper place.

I learned from Morris: Hookers are smart. They get paid in advance.

But in another way, even though he wouldn't speak to me either, his therapy was a success. He would only let the hookers blow him. Me, he fucked.

•   •   •

why I stayed married: **reason #3**

MY HUSBAND HAS a rough, handsome, professorial kind of face, but more than any other adjective that could be used to describe it, the one that fits best is "sad." When I look at him, it is as if I am at the ASPCA peering in a window, seeing all the unadopted puppies and kittens and desperately wanting to save them. I want to cradle them all. I want to cradle my husband.

I tease my husband about his sad face. I call him my little clown. I run my tongue along the scars. He tells me his face has grown sad from years of worry. "How many years?" I ask. He tells me that he started worrying at three. He says that he remembers the first day anyone noticed. His dad used to make pancakes every Sunday morning for him and his brothers. One day, after breakfast, his brothers went out to play while he stayed at the table, his face between his hands.

His father asked, "Are you sick?"

He replied, "No."

His father asked, "Did something happen?"

Again, his answer was, "No."

"Well then," his dad said, "what's wrong?"

He answered, "I'm worried."

"What are you worried about?" his father asked.

"I'm just worried," he replied as easily as a child might say, "I'm hungry."

"But, what are you worried about?" his father asked again.

"Everything," he answered. "I'm worried about everything."

What should I do with my grown husband to wipe away the worries he's been collecting since he was three? I tell him bad jokes and use funny voices till I make him smile. When he smiles, I feel as if I have rescued every animal in the ASPCA.

chapter 4

Suffer Along with Me

*M*y third husband was duped. Fifteen years ago, he fell in love with and married a singer with a life much like his, except that he was kind of famous and she was kind of not.

We sipped Rémy Martin and traded stories about the music business. He told me about working with Chet Baker when Chet Baker's heroin habit was at its worst, and they had to stop in a terrible section of Harlem to buy a bag before a gig. Chet kept mumbling, "My wife nees her medicine. My wife nees her medicine," as they pulled the van over and Chet stumbled out.

I told him about the night when our piano player had a

grand mal seizure on stage. We slid him under the piano as he shit in his pants, and the saxophone player seamlessly moved to the piano stool in the middle of me singing Hoagy Carmichael's "Skylark."

He told me about the time the famous lead singer brought his mistress to Paris on the gig, and they were kissing in the green room when the singer's wife surprised him with an unexpected transatlantic flight. As she walked into the green room unannounced, my husband spotted her and grabbed the mistress in his arms, successfully pretending that she was *his* girlfriend.

I told him about a great bald-as-a-doorknob trombone player who had played in the big band era. The bandleader told him that he looked too old, so he might start hiring him less. At the next gig, the trombone player opened his trombone case, pulled out his trombone stand, set it up, pulled out his bow tie, put it on, pulled out his trombone, put it together, pulled out his new black toupee, and slapped it on his head. When the gig ended, he reversed the entire process, and exited the room.

At the time, I was living in Boston, singing with a sixteen-piece swing orchestra. We did fancy jobs—Liv Ullmann's second wedding, Michael Dukakis's inaugural balls, and, most impressive of all in the retelling, Red Auerbach's retirement party and the two ticker-tape parades through Boston after the Celtics won the championship. It sounds great, and it was. Except that I worked for notoriously cheap bandleaders. We were never paid one cent over union scale. Because the union scale was higher if you drove your car, the bandleaders made us pile into their cars like circus clowns, and, laughing gleefully, the guys would fart up a storm as we drove to work.

Meanwhile, my husband was living in New York City, where he worked for one of the most famous musicians in the world, in one of the most famous jazz clubs in the world. Back then, I'd visit him every chance I got—sometimes leaving for New York when my gig ended at midnight. I thought nothing of making the four-hour drive at that time. We'd stay up all night, go for breakfast at 5 a.m., mess around, drink more Rémy Martin and black coffee, and wear sunglasses to hide our puffy eyes. When I went to see him play, the audience might also hold the likes of Sarah Vaughan, Van Morrison, Joni Mitchell, Tommy Flanagan, or Kenny Barron.

My husband thought he'd finally found someone who could understand his life of sleeping late and practicing. He was right. At that point in my life, nothing bothered me. I was high on the East Village where he lived, and I was high on jazz. We would listen over and over to Serge Chaloff's baritone sax solo on "Body and Soul," and I would almost pass out with pleasure. I thought I'd finally found a way out of Boston and into New York City, my lifelong dream.

One Monday afternoon, while I was visiting him, I picked up the yellow pages and looked at listings for music. I saw an ad for Peter Duchin's orchestra. I'd heard of them. I was feeling brazenly confident because in Boston I was at the top of my game. I called the Peter Duchin office and asked for work.

"Send us a demo tape and a photo," the booker on the end of the line said.

"Look," I told him. "Anyone can walk into a studio and make a great-sounding demo tape. What I can do is call ten Cole Porter tunes in a row and jump in without missing a measure. You can't put *that* on a demo tape. So give me a night. If you don't like what I do, stop me after sixteen bars, shake my hand, and send me home. I can take it."

As I heard myself speak, I wanted to blurt out, "I made it up. Goodbye." Before I could do that, though, the booker gave me a job the following night at the Waldorf Astoria. After that night, he gave me more.

I called my bandleader in Boston and quit on the spot. In 1987, I moved to New York to live with my third husband-to-be in the East Village apartment he'd lived in for fifteen years before we met—the apartment where everything seemed so romantic.

THE SEWER DRAIN for the building was located right under the bed in our basement apartment.

The drain attracted strange little fleas and flies.

I was beginning to feel like Pig-Pen, but less content.

One night, a large roach sprinted across my face, and I screamed.

Then, the sewer backed up.

The rats—did I mention there were rats?—could be heard chewing the insulation in the walls.

The streets were decorated with dog turds, human turds, and walking turds—otherwise known as drug dealers.

I remember the first time I saw a grown man squat on the street and take a dump.

I remember the first time I opened the refrigerator and found it filled with dead flies.

I remember when my husband put a pan over a giant cockroach on the kitchen counter and left it there for days because he didn't want to hurt the insect.

"Everyone in New York lives like this," he told me, as he lit his morning "wake up" joint. "Rats and roaches are a fact of New York life."

How much work did it take on my part to believe this? Not that rats and roaches existed, but that we had to live so close to them? The apartment hadn't changed since all those previous times I'd visited him. What part of me never noticed? What part of me thought I wanted to live like this?

Ever the optimist, I dyed my hair East Village–interplanetary-blonde and shopped in thrift stores. I let my dark roots grow in. I ripped holes in my tights. I tried to get into it.

The bathroom in the apartment was so old that the walls had crumbled and the floor was erupting like the Badlands—the tiling bubbling up with no support underneath. You could almost see the limestone era and the oil era of the planet. One day, while I was putting my makeup on in front of the mirror, a neighbor who was walking down the hall yelled out, "Mornin', cute-toes." You could see my feet from the hallway because of the big holes in the walls.

I wanted to call the super and make him fix the hole. "It's the building's job to fix it," I insisted.

"But they won't do it right," my husband countered. "They'll just cover it over. I want it done right. I need to examine this more closely to understand the underlying cause."

"The underlying cause?" I yelled. "A goddamn stranger just started a conversation about my feet!"

My husband wouldn't budge.

He wanted to fix it right.

He bought books about how to fix things.

He lit a joint and read the books.

He lit a joint and examined the crumbling walls.

He lit a joint and ordered fried chicken and ate it while he meditated on the crater in the floor.

He developed surprising theories about drywall and tiling.

But he never fixed anything. The books became another pile lying around the apartment.

Enraged, I found a board on the street.

I carried it into the apartment.

I put it over the floor.

He picked it up and carried it back outside.

I bought cement.

He returned it.

I carried in the board and put it in front of the hole in the wall.

He took it down.

I cried, and we broke up over the bathroom.

HOWEVER, MY AMBIVALENCE forced me to rent the apartment across the hall from him, although I claimed it was because it was vacant and finding space in New York City is hard. We would yell back and forth and kick each other's doors. I had good reason to be mad. The heating pipes for the entire building were in my apartment, so I had relocated from a sewer to a sauna.

EVENTUALLY, WE BROKE up long enough that I started to write my first book and got the notion to go to social work school for credibility. I was still singing, but one day I was talking about John Coltrane's solo on "Like Someone in Love," and the next day I was diagnosing John Coltrane with every personality disorder in the *Diagnostic and Statistical Manual*. Upon entering social work school, I suddenly saw dysfunction everywhere, and said so as calmly as Coltrane counted off "A Love Supreme."

I fondly remember the night I used my fledgling diagnostic skills to call my husband passive-aggressive. Mixing his rare wit with his anger, he yelled at the top of his lungs:

"NOW, I'M AGGRESSIVE-AGGRESSIVE! DO YOU LIKE THAT BETTER?"

WE TANGLED IN this cellar like bull elk that lock horns. They fight until they are exhausted. They panic. They fall. They discover they can't unlock their horns. In this position, they starve to death.

We would have continued to survive this way except that a friend offered to let us take over his lease in a much bigger, much nicer space. When he showed us his apartment, we couldn't get over how lovely it was—with a big pillar in the middle of the living room, and long, huge windows everywhere. There were copper pots hanging in the kitchen, a love seat, and willowy, off-white curtains with fancy rods.

We jumped at the chance. But the bastard took all his furniture with him when he moved. We arrived at an empty space.

And did we ask for tips from the folks at the local furniture store?

Did we join the masses at Ikea?

No. Instead, we converted the place into a storage unit filled with amplifiers, books, and fifty never-to-be-emptied cardboard boxes. We carted our ramshackle boards and musty furniture from our last dump. The twenty-year-old futon, the night table I'd found on the street, the hand-me-down towels, the scummy wok, the mismatched silver, the paperboard bookcases with the paperboard peeling. We set it up, and guess what? This place looked exactly like our last dump, only larger.

What else could we do? We could barely afford the rent in the new place. Sinclair fired me. Morris fired me—not that he'd ever paid me anyway. Everything I made was going toward renting the smelly office. Meanwhile, my husband was gambling stocks on margin and going deeper and deeper into debt—$25,000, $30,000, $35,000 and rising.

I needed money, and I was clueless about how to get it. Until I met Eve, who showed up and taught me what I needed to know.

EVE DROVE A top-of-the-line Mercedes, wore a full-length mink, and lived in a huge home in Hamilton Township, New Jersey, but couldn't afford to heat her house. "I'm sleeping under pelts," she told me, as if she were saying, "I'm sleeping in a dumpster."

Her ex-husband was not making his alimony payments and was being investigated by the FBI. He hid his money offshore. "And the dickhead swears he only has two pennies to his name." He refused to give Eve one penny on principle, but since he had no principles, it was one more way to bully Eve. She was wearing Chanel but eating corn flakes for breakfast, lunch, and dinner.

With Eve, I decided to use the technique of self-psychology, which meant that I would try to help her nurture herself, since others had clearly let her down. When I asked her how she might nurture herself, Eve told me that she wanted a face-lift to go with her eye lift, an erection for her impotent boyfriend with the obvious toupee, and an allowance from her narcissistic Palm Beach mother, Ida. Heretofore, Ida had refused to give her anything because, even though Ida had a lot of money, she thought she might live to be 125, so she'd need all the money for herself.

Eve also had the idea that she could nurture herself by getting a reduced fee from me. "You know, I drive all the way in from New Jersey to see you. I park the car in a *lot*. Do you really think that I can afford to do that? It's a huge sacrifice. You can't even know." I imagined Eve giving up one of her cereal meals so she could pay for gas to come to Manhattan. When Eve switched to a seductive baby-talk voice to describe being alone, huddled under mink, I reduced my fee to just this side of paying her to be my patient. I thought it was a reparative gesture in a lifetime of people letting her down. It showed her that I cared about her, that I wasn't trying to take advantage of her.

WHEN EVE THREW in the baby talk, I was seared with a deep shame. It wasn't that I occasionally resorted to baby talk with my husband, but that baby talk was the *only* way I spoke to him. Like Morris, he wanted blow jobs all the time, or, at least, hand jobs. And, like with Morris, I had great difficulty mustering empathy for his needs. I couldn't feel that his desires had anything to do with me. So I did the only thing my unconscious could think of—I talked like a three-year-old. Once it started, I couldn't stop. Because when I was three, I was happier, definitely happier.

. . .

IT WAS WEEKS later when I began to notice how Eve was always freshly manicured and had her hair frosted regularly and came in carrying a "grande" cappuccino from a designer java joint. That cappuccino must have cost $3.95. I've only permitted myself a few cappuccinos in my whole life because of the outrageous prices. I've never understood how people can spend $5 for a coffee, $10 for a manicure, and $1.25 for a bottle of water without giving it a second thought. I can't permit myself such luxury items without extended scrutiny. What was I thinking when I, who talked like a baby and lived in a dump, dipped my fee below sea level?

SOME WEEKS, EVE railed about her boyfriend's limp penis. "I call the dickhead 'el limp dick-o,'" she snarled, throwing back her head and laughing bitterly. Other weeks, she fell into a victim stupor. "Uuugh," she moaned, insisting she needed a prescription for Valium. When I recommended a psychopharmacologist who could give her an evaluation for antidepressant medication, she perked up. "Is he cute?"

Often, she showed me her hysterectomy scar, her cesarean scar, the scar on her wrist where she had made an itty-bitty cut to see how it would feel, and she pulled her eyelids up to show me the faint scars from her previous eye lift. "Getting this eye lift was like buying a new couch and putting it in a room filled with old furniture. All it does is make the old furniture look older. The face-lift is not optional. Did I show you the scar from when I fell off the motor scooter in Bermuda?"

Eve cried because her ex-husband's new wife looked like a younger version of her. She cried, "I haven't had full penetration in years." She cried because her impotent, hairless boyfriend was dating other women whom he was also unable to fuck.

I said, "If you really need to date a shithead, maybe you can find a shithead who can keep an erection."

She asked me if I'd help her write a personal ad. "Stiff dick, fat wallet," she said, tickled with herself. But she never brought it up again.

Instead of seeking out a decent guy, Eve pined for the creepy one.

Instead of staying warm at a friend's house, she slept in an unheated house.

Instead of enjoying her beautiful face at fifty, she wept for her beautiful face at thirty.

Instead of taking a job to earn money, she searched for a cheaper bagel.

Eve was the first to RSVP to the engraved invitation to suffering.

She didn't set out to be miserable, so why, at every corner where she might have stepped away from misery, did she instead take the same old turn that pointed her back?

Observing Eve's tailspin into masochism became increasingly difficult for me, because nothing I said or didn't say, nothing I did or didn't do, seemed to help. It was not easy for me to hear "and then . . . and then . . . and then . . ." week after week and feel so totally ineffective, as if I had no impact on her life at all.

Was she looking for a witness or a therapist? Did she need me to be a bad therapist for her, one more in her long line of disappointments?

Something else about Eve's misery needled me. I couldn't pinpoint it, but when she walked through the door, I started to feel critical of her. Then I started to dislike her. Then I started to hate her.

I hated her fresh manicure. I hated the tissue she pulled out of her red leather tissue case. I hated her perfect blonde streaks. I hated her measly check. I hated her when I walked into my messy apartment where my husband had thrown everything around looking for his bass wheel again. I hated her while I was picking all the shit up off the floor, realizing the useless battle I'd soon be having. I hated her while my husband swigged cognac out of a bottle as he theorized about online gambling and lost more money. I hated her because my apartment was a shit hole and my furniture was sub-firewood and she wasn't paying me. I hated her because my marriage had not improved my life-style one bit.

I hated her because my husband never brought me flowers, not one fucking flower, in years. I hated her because I wrote a book that people were buying, but I still wasn't making enough money. Mostly, I hated her because every time she did the blind man's walk into masochism, she bumped right into me. There we were, dangling side by side on the disappointment daisy chain—neither one of us doing a goddamned thing to improve our lots.

I'd had it. I was going to bring up my fee again. Meanwhile, she started counting change to see if she had enough for the gasoline to get home. Feeling my fury rise, I swallowed it back and decided to use a technique from the feminist school of relational psychotherapy, which is focused on how much happier women are when they are economically in control and earning money. I asked Eve if she'd considered nurturing herself *and* me by getting a job.

She flung her change back in her purse and said, "A job? You think I should get a job? Look, darling. You're not doing your job."

"What is my job?" I asked, surprised at the vehemence of her affect.

She looked at me as if I were daft and, with more than a little condescension, replied firmly, "Do you really think you're coming up with ideas I haven't thought of before? Do you really think it never occurred to me that I could work or stay at a friend's or sell my fucking car? Nurture, schmurture. I am not paying you to make suggestions. I am not paying you to help me job-hunt. I'm not paying you to solve my problems. I'm paying you to do *one thing and one thing only.*"

She let it out slowly, each syllable suspended in midair like one of the unfortunate Flying Wallendas.

"WHAT I'm paying you to do, ALL I'm paying you to do, is SUF-FER-A-LONG-WITH-ME."

Time stood still.

Eve, not Freud, enlightened me to the fact that I could earn a living doing what I'd been doing my whole life. Who feels sorrier for herself than I do? Who can't seem ever to get it right in spite of a lifetime of therapy, therapy, therapy? Who *actually became* a therapist and still doesn't feel better? Who can understand the life span from infancy to adulthood because she spends much of her time as a baby? Plus, who has experienced more whiners or listened to more sufferers than I have, since people like me tend to find each other? I'm on the executive board of whiners and sufferers as we decline, decay, degenerate, grumble, snivel, whimper, mewl, endure, lament, dwindle, and droop.

That night, when my husband picked me up, I couldn't wait to tell him about my revelation: All I had to do to make a living for the second half of my life was to charge money for what I'd done for free in the first half. And all we had to do to be happy was to stop suffering along with each other and grow up.

The next day, I introduced myself to every person in every office on my floor. I visited the young chiropractor, mentioning that I had a backache and would call him soon. I called my friends and asked them to send their friends to me, reminding them that they owed me for counseling them all these years for free. I brought my business cards to my hairdresser, explaining how I'd need to get more business or else stop coloring my hair.

My practice began to grow.

. . .

why I stayed married: **reason #4**

IN THE LIVING room, my husband would pull his big, beautiful, chocolate-colored double bass out of the case. A lush sculpture, a museum piece with five, fat strings. I loved to listen to him play. I loved it when he ran his horse-hair bow over the strings. I loved it when his big, flat fingers flew with confidence and grace.

And his solos. You cannot imagine his solos. Year after year after year, I've listened to musicians solo. I can even sing a few of the miraculous famous ones. But so many solos aren't great or original or clearly thought out. My husband's were. He composed little separate tunes inside his solos. They had beginnings, middles, and ends. Like little stories, tales from the gifted.

When he played the bass, he had a little smile that showed his perfect, white teeth—not a filling in sight. How many times had I fallen in love when he picked up that bass? How many times had I fallen in love with that smile, which I'd noticed the first time I saw him?

Once, he got a recording date where he was going to play jazz solos over Rachmaninoff. There, in the living room, day after day, I'd listen to Rachmaninoff as he practiced along. Sometimes I sat on the floor at his feet. Sometimes I danced around him. Sometimes I danced naked.

Sometimes he put the bass down and took me in his arms while Rachmaninoff swept through the room.

chapter 5

The Family Tree

What has to happen for two parents to raise three pedophiles? One in a family is mind-boggling, two seems impossible, but three? Now, think. Are there other children in the family? When you learn about a pedophile, do you wonder if he had a baby brother—or perhaps a doll-faced sister?

Danny, my gentle, crane-folding teacher, was one of five other children. Danny, with a top-shelf laugh that slides through you. Danny, working the night shift, taking Japanese lessons during the day. Danny, who spoke so quietly during those first few sessions that I had to move my chair closer and closer, until I began to think he wanted to sit in my lap. I told you he'd come to see me once before because he was being bullied, but it was more than that.

Yes. You are beginning to think about him differently now. Perhaps there are other reasons that would make a grown man fold tiny pieces of paper over and over again.

I have seen this before—expansive souls who begin to shrink. A splendid artist who once made huge sculptures ends up laboring over tiny, Italian mosaic tiles. A research scientist, once a boy who loved dinosaurs, ends up focusing on the wing patterns of fruit bats. A laughing girl who once donated the proceeds of her lemonade stand to charity ends up selling pharmaceutical supplies, counting pills, writing and rewriting numbers on a spreadsheet, and paying a nightly visit to her good friend, Jack Daniel's. What terrors squeeze a heart into small, indistinguishable capsules? What nightmares lead a laughing girl to be soothed by 80 proof? And what about Alice? Did she fall through the looking glass or was she pushed?

Danny's fiancée never made it to the United States. In the end, she didn't want him enough. Years later, he found yet another woman who didn't want him. He was captured by an unrequited crush on Rose, who worked a printing machine near his. "After work, she likes to go to Sammy's because she likes to play pool. She drinks too much. She gets sick. I go with her. I don't want her walking home alone. When I put her to bed, I can usually tell if I'm gonna have to cover for her the next day."

Two or three times a week, Danny would do the same

thing—help Rose to the bathroom, clean her up, carry her to the couch. Before she nodded out, she'd remind him that the chemistry wasn't right.

What was I supposed to do about Danny's overarching pull toward a love that included the regular wiping up of vomit? Was I supposed to help him win her, or was I supposed to talk him out of her?

I wanted to know his family tree. I did this with every patient, rigorously recording people, events, and years in a drawing called a genogram, a social worker's family map. There were little pen marks for everything—love, conflict, death, divorce.

As I sat with Danny, this simple family map that I was supposed to draw wasn't coming out right. I couldn't understand what Danny was telling me, and I didn't know why. I kept confusing his brothers and sisters and who was what age. To this day, I'm still not sure where Danny came in sibling order. By the end of the session, I was still unable to extract even the simplest details of how many brothers and sisters he had, who lived where, how they got along, when they grew up, and what they were doing now. I didn't understand why I didn't understand. Was it me? Was it because I only had two sisters, and I wasn't used to keeping track of big families with lots of children?

The next week, I started over again, but I still couldn't hear what Danny was saying. What was blocking my ears? *Laurie is married to whom? Brian does what?* I couldn't hold any of it.

"Can this really be that complicated?" I asked Danny.

"I'm going to Paris," he replied.

I told him I'd love to talk about Paris, but why go to the doctor with a bleeding wound if you're planning to tell her what good movies you've seen lately? The doctor needs information related to her job in order to do her job. So does a psychotherapist. Why was he resisting giving me my supplies?

He skipped his next appointment.

He was very late for the one after that.

"I slept with two brothers in a bed, head to toe, head to toe," he announced. "We had one bathroom for all of us. Brian took me in the bathroom. He made me suck him off and tell him sex stories. I was seven. He broke my glasses."

Like lightning, Brian shoved himself down my throat, too.

I sat still. I am paid *not* to gag. Danny told me he went to confession to tell the priest. The priest tried to put his penis down Danny's throat, too. (I wrote down and deleted this last sentence twenty times. If this had been fiction, it would have been too much.)

FOR ME, IT started when I was eight because of a messy basement. I read love comics and movie magazines down there, and I didn't pick them up off the floor. There were the wedding photos of Eddie Fisher and Debby Reynolds. *The Mysterians*, a movie with aliens, was coming into the theaters near me. One day, I pulled my mother's wedding gown out of the box in the boiler room and tried it on. Meanwhile, my mother was yelling at me from the kitchen. She needed to go grocery shopping, and she couldn't go when there was junk all over the cellar floor. But I couldn't clean up while I was wearing a wedding gown.

Just then, my father's best friend drove up our driveway in his janitor clothes, smoking his gross pipe. My mother told me years later that he did not believe in brushing his teeth. They were covered in a green-and-black film from years of pipe tobacco and neglect.

He said to my mother, "Go shopping. When you come home, the basement will be spotless."

He opened the cellar door, and he locked the door from the inside. It had a slide lock.

Why?

Why would a cellar door have a slide lock on the inside?

DANNY IS SOBBING so hard that I can't understand what he is telling me. My eardrums do a Haitian voodoo dance. I can't hear Danny because the blood is pounding so loudly in my ears.

And then I hear.

Brian, the bully brother, was broken in by Eddie, the oldest. Manny was the baby, and everyone did him. And all Manny can think about are little girls, so he sticks his fingers in electrical sockets, fries his brains for fun, drives his bicycle into a moving truck, and jumps out of a window, but doesn't die. Nothing stops the thoughts.

The bully brother takes Danny's little sister into the bed with the two other boys. The bully says that if they don't hold her down, he'll kill them, that if they tell, he'll kill the little sister, he'll kill the parents.

I am eight years old and locked in the basement. Danny's little sister was littler than me. There were three of them on her.

Where is she now?

Does she sleep?

How old are her children?

Is this why I don't have any?

I try to run up the steps past him, tripping on the hem of the wedding gown, and, as I stand at the top of these steps trying to unlock the door, he rises slowly, puffing and smiling. I begin banging on the cellar door, even though I know that no one is there.

No one is ever there.

When my husband comes at me for sex, he is too rough. He grabs me. I tell him to be gentle, but he is a big, rough bear. He knows nothing of gentle. He wants me. He won't take no for an answer. I am trapped on the cellar stairs.

YEARS LATER, A therapist tried to tell me that part of my problem was that I liked what my father's best friend did to me, and that I felt guilty for liking it. But, I didn't. He hurt me many times. He grabbed my wrist in the meanest way. He didn't worry if I scratched myself on his belt. This was the good part for him.

What he *liked* was hurting me. What I liked was that I never said ouch. And I never cried. I never gave him the satisfaction. Even today, if *I* cry *he* wins.

I didn't think my husband cared. He wanted what he wanted. I talked baby talk. I talked fast. I talked a lot. I made him stop.

EACH PEDOPHILE-BROTHER HAD a different story. The bully brother made children suck him because he could. He fucked them and then hit them. Breaking Danny's glasses was not a mistake. Today, the bully brother is married with two children. He does not fuck and punch children anymore. The same cannot be said for his wife.

The baby brother murders himself, inch by inch. He's lost two fingers. He's broken almost every bone at least once. But he has not been able to break the thing inside that wants only young girls. He keeps himself injured so he cannot act on his urges.

One afternoon, the oldest brother waited for a younger boy behind the bookmobile. Danny's family ended up paying that boy's family off for what happened that afternoon. How did this exchange go? "OK, your sixteen-year-old son made my nine-year-old son suck his dick. That's worth five thousand dollars." What did they tell their son? "This is the only way we can pay for your braces." It's hard to imagine.

I TELL MY husband.

One day, I say, "He locked me in the cellar."

It wasn't that my parents didn't listen.

It was that linchpin moment when I could see how inconvenient I was.

I was a chafed thigh on a hot summer day, something small and irritating that you don't want to be bothered with yet cannot ignore.

My husband insists that I revisit this with my mother. He thinks it is the only way I will heal and he can get the sex he wants. He is so practical that way.

So I tell my mother, who does not remember having heard this before but says she is not surprised. This man who was my father's best friend tried to molest another girl. She remembers that.

It never comes up again.

I blame my husband for bringing me to this place.

I EXPLAIN TO Danny that it is my job to protect children. I am mandated by law to notify the authorities whenever I learn anything in my practice that constitutes child abuse. After much talking, Danny gives me his parents' address and the name of the town that his oldest brother, Eddie, who is still an active pedophile, lives in.

I call the Bureau of Child Welfare in the town where Eddie lives.

They tell me to call the Bureau of Child Welfare in the town where Eddie did bad things.

I do. But I don't have the name of any of the victims and Danny refuses to permit me to give his name, saying that it would kill his parents.

The Bureau of Child Welfare tells me to call the police in the town that Eddie lives in.

I do. The police tell me to call the police in the town Eddie came from.

I do. They say that without the name of a victim my call is hearsay.

I ask if they could at least call him and tell him they know where he is. Or, go to the parents and ask for their help. They say they cannot do anything without the name of a victim or without Danny.

Basically, they are all telling me the same thing: If the victim will not come forward, if I can't name names, there is nothing they can or will do.

I call the National Association of Social Workers Ethics Committee for guidance. Their answering machine tells me not to leave a message there because no one will call me back, but it gives me no other instructions. I call back and ask the receptionist to reconnect me to a person. She reconnects me to the machine.

Danny calls a family meeting and finds out that the oldest brother, Eddie, made his niece suck his dick, too. She was three. The parents insist on silence, saying it is a family problem.

I call all the authorities, start all over again, and get the same response all over again. Without Danny's testimony, without the paid-off children or their families, without the niece who was three and is now seventeen with a baby of her own, there is nothing they can do.

Danny and I are statistics, chatter over martinis, the six o'clock news. Kids who don't tell. We sleep like cattle dreaming of hot iron. We keep the family secrets. We are the fleshy babies of mothers with whiteout eyes. We are some jolly uncle's favorite Junior Miss.

MY HUSBAND STOPS reaching for me, and he begins to watch even more porn. Who can blame him? For me, every porno tape left in the player is another assault. I turn on Channel Two at seven and up pop three women smothering and licking every nook and cranny of one man. He is assaulting me, isn't he? My marriage is happening in a basement.

MY JOB IS not for everyone. You have to be able to hear the unspeakable and keep a perspective on your own unspeakables. You have to live your life knowing that you can't always protect the children. You cannot force Danny to go to the police. You have to be able to have someone's penis shoved down your throat in one second and still be pleasant company for your husband in the next. And you have to watch a family pull tighter than a sailor's knot when pedophiles become uncles.

What has to happen for two parents to raise three pedophiles? I still don't know.

But I do know that, when work is over, I want to leave Danny's family in my office and do things that take my mind off my work.

Like last night—my girlfriend took me to a concert at Carnegie Hall because her boyfriend was too sick to go. The tickets were for the Christmas performance of the Vienna Boys' Choir. As I listened to the sweet boy voices and smiled at the chubby boy in the front row with a soprano that could end a war, I began to notice the tops of the heads of the people who were seated in the orchestra section. I thought, but wasn't sure, that there were several men who seemed to have come alone. And I thought they seemed a little more mesmerized than the rest of us. Then, when the very last song had ended, I noticed two of these men, who had paid top dollar to sit so close to the stage, seemed lost in private reveries. As the boys trailed off the stage, one of these men appeared to be weeping. The other forgot to clap.

. . .

why i stayed married: **reason #5**

WE GO TO all the children's movies together. Every pig, every cub, every dancing elephant—we've seen them all. When we go hiking, my husband sets the pace by loudly singing a song from *Dumbo* about pink elephants on parade.

When *The Little Mermaid* came out, we sang, "Under the Sea." When *Beauty and the Beast* came out, we held each other tightly all through it.

One morning, before he leaves for work, my husband tells me, "I have a surprise," and he leads me into the living room. He hits the tape player that is set at Angela Lansbury's version of "Beauty and the Beast." My husband puts out his arms, inviting me to dance, and swirls me around the living room floor in my old T-shirt and bare feet.

My head is on his shoulder. The joy and the pain are exquisite. We are hopeful. We may get through our childhoods after all.

chapter 6

A Bed That Told the Truth

*L*et me explain our sex life. During the eight official years of my marriage, my husband and I had sex three times. Two of the times I remember. The third—well, I'm guessing there were three. In the first few drafts of writing this book, I left our sex life out, putting myself through hoops to do so. I didn't want to hurt my husband. I didn't want to shame him or to shame myself.

It does seem shameful, at the least. Humiliating. Inexplicable, surely.

There is a code among those of us in sexless marriages, and the code is "don't tell." But if I don't tell you, this story won't make as much sense as if I do tell you.

Before we were married, we lived together for seven years, so I think of our marriage as fifteen years. We did have sex at first. I remember thinking at the end of our first year of dating that I still enjoyed making love with him just as much as ever. There was the night in my Boston apartment when we were boiling adzuki beans in the kitchen and he took me on the kitchen counter. There was the first time in his apartment, after we came home from his gig at the Village Vanguard, when I felt as hip as I would ever feel. Oh, those late nights when I watched him on stage with his hands all over that bass, and I imagined what those fast fingers would feel like on me. Our lovemaking was happy.

Then, he took down the board I'd put up in the bathroom to hide my toes.

Next, he went off on a European tour, and, while he was traveling, I rifled through his boxes. No one snoops to find secret theater tickets. We snoop to find what I found: a letter confessing that he'd cheated on me when he was in Japan. He wrote that it happened on the very morning I'd made my first international call to Japan—that the woman was still in his room when I called him.

Then, I found fleas and flies in his refrigerator.

The final straw came when the phone bill contained 1-900 phone calls. On the dates I'd been teaching my flirting seminars in Boston, he'd been having phone sex in New York.

I thought my husband was a predator.

I freaked out. I cut myself, smeared the blood on the

phone bills, and stuck them into the walls with kitchen knives.

This led to a phase of no sex.

Many couples have phases of no sex.

Our phase lasted thirteen years.

In the beginning, he protested mightily. Soon he let up, and, after a while, he appeared even less interested than I was.

There was so much we couldn't work out in this adult relationship. Still, we loved each other, so we reconfigured our lives, leaving out sex. We confined ourselves to secret masturbation as our adult sexuality changed from something hopeful to something old and awful.

I shifted to a time and place where I could be unsexually blissful. I became the three-year-old to whom nothing bad had yet happened. He tried to join me there, but he was such a sad, sad boy. We bought stuffed animals and named them. There was Mr. Buffalo, Mr. Bear, and Baby Baby Baby Bear. He took Mr. Bear on tour with him to Japan. We took them all on a road trip to Florida, careful not to leave them in the hot car overnight. We made up whole albums of songs about our family. We remained deeply in love with each other this way, and I got out of the cellar.

WHEN MY HUSBAND proposed to me, we hadn't had sex in two years. When we got married, we hadn't had sex in four. We went for it once on our honeymoon in Paris and had a perfectly delightful time, and once more when we got back home. Both times, we wondered why we'd stopped.

You can't hide in bed.

Not from the past, not from the present, not from each other.

Neither of us was prepared for a bed that told the truth.

But there was this one time . . . I was leaving for an overnight singing gig in Pennsylvania. He offered to drive me. On the long ride there, I began to talk about my childhood, and I began to cry. I told him all kinds of things that no one knew—about my father's best friend, about things I'll discuss later in this book.

After my gig, we made love in our hotel room, and, for the first time, we found the way into each other. Maybe this was because I didn't try to push him away or hide when he gave me pleasure. I felt or I allowed myself to feel for the first time that he was enjoying it. I helped him. It was the first time I had an orgasm with him. I said "I love you, I love you, I love you" a thousand times.

When we drove home, I wept almost the whole way, and I had my head on his shoulder.

The next day, I left for a vacation at my sister's in California.

When I came home, it was to an apartment filled with filthy dishes, rotten food, and dust. I banished my husband to the couch in the living room.

"You know why you're doing this," he protested. "Because we got too close and you got too scared."

I never came back to him as a grown-up again, not in any real way. He, for his part, barricaded himself with enough junk to keep me away for the rest of our lives.

TODAY, I UNDERSTAND. In the hotel room, it was just us. No gambling debt, no fleas and flies, no crash pad full of boxes, no crazy families, no pot, no father's best friend, no boarded up bathrooms, no doing and undoing.

To keep the spirit of the hotel room alive, we'd have to change our world outside the hotel room.

We'd have to bring the hotel room into the rest of our lives.

Or the rest of our lives into the hotel room.

The hotel room was enchanted.

The spell only worked when we were there.

.   .   .

why I stayed married: **reason #6**

WHEN MY HUSBAND bought both of us hats with mosquito netting that could fold down to cover one's entire head, I laughed at him. The hats looked so stupid. I told him that not only would I not wear mine, I would pretend I didn't know him if he wore his.

Months later, we were deep in the woods of Harriman State Park, following a trail to a lake we'd seen on a map. The terrain got muddy, then muddier, then came almost to our boot tops, but I wanted to see this lake because sometimes we would come upon species of ducks and birds that I'd never seen before.

Out of nowhere, a swarm of mosquitoes descended upon us like wedding guests on the buffet line. I couldn't swat fast enough.

My husband opened his backpack.

He pulled out his stupid hat.

He rolled down the netting.

And he gave his hat to me.

chapter 7

My Husband Gets Shoe Polish on the Couch

*E*ventually, Eve sold her big suburban house and bought a small apartment on the Upper East Side. She carted in her wallpaper samples to show me, gushing about the groin appeal of the paperhanger. Danny redecorated his apartment in a Japanese style with low furniture and rice screens, and was even sleeping on a tatami mat. Several of my other patients went to department stores, auctions, and flea markets, reporting on everything from new silverware to a couch that had to be returned because it wouldn't fit through the door. My patients were moving on with their lives.

After years of absorbing everyone else's tastes in décor,

I began to notice something I'd never noticed before: my environment. Other people didn't live like I lived. They had coffee tables and friends over for dinner. Ross and his wife, Mary, invited us to their house for dinner, and I sat dumbstruck. They had real paintings on the walls. They did not eat off kitchen counters. They had vintage martini glasses.

Moreover, it seemed that other people threw spoiled food away instead of leaving it in the refrigerator because it was your husband's spoiled food and he was supposed to be the one to throw it away, except he never did.

As if awakening from a coma, I became aware of comforters, woven rugs, colorful accents. There were matching sheets to be had in every color whenever you wanted them. There were tables in every kind of wood, every kind of height. And baskets—baskets made of banana leaves that could hold the things currently piled on the floor. There were loosely woven curtains that let in the light but protected your privacy. Not everyone streaked naked from the living room to the bedroom because there were no curtains.

How could I be so close to fifty and not have known this before? I'd certainly been in my share of nice homes, but the idea of making a home never occurred to me—perhaps because home had always felt like it was one step from the boiler room. I had noticed the dirt in our house, and I hated it. I had noticed the boxes. But I'd only thought about cleaning and getting rid of the boxes. I never thought about what might be there instead.

Nonetheless, I woke up one morning yearning for new

sponges. New sheets. I wanted place mats (but first I had to get a table). I decided to buy a couch. In all our years together, we'd never had a couch, never even looked through a magazine for one.

"I want a couch," I announced.

This comment led to the same disaster we had when, two years before, I had said, "I want a Mini-Vac." My husband insisted that I wait until he could check *Consumer Reports* to find the best Min-Vac. Months later, he still hadn't checked. Finally, I went out and bought a Mini-Vac for $29.99. He returned it the next day so he could buy a better one. A year later, we still didn't have one.

Whatever I did, he undid.

Doing and undoing was our life.

We fought about the couch for months. We could not agree on a day to look for one. When we finally went to look for one, we could not agree on size or shape or filling or price. We spent hours in the couch department, only to leave without a couch.

I wanted to go to Bloomingdale's and pick out something on sale. He wanted a luxury, handcrafted, down-filled sofa. He thought our couch should last a lifetime. I thought maybe the tide was turning. I saw his wish for a lovely couch as a positive development. Maybe the era of doing and undoing was over. Maybe now we were doing and doing. I thought, maybe, if we could complete the purchase of a couch, we'd end feeling married and staying married after all.

Little did I know, as we flipped through fabric choices, that a splendid, off-white, goose down-filled classic sofa was going to be my ticket to unmitigated lunacy.

First, like Eve's eye lift, the new couch made the rest of our place look shittier than it already did—if that was possible. The chipped fake-wood bookcases looked more chipped and more fake. The scraped floors looked more scraped. The dust bunnies looked like dust dinosaurs. The smelly boxes piled around the house smelled even worse.

Within one week, the unthinkable happened: I noticed a thin, black band along the front skirt of the sofa. Examining it closely, I started hyperventilating. I pointed it out to my husband, who said, "How should I know?"

Several nights later, I saw him pick up the paper, go to the couch, sit down, and thrust his newly polished black tuxedo shoes flush against the skirt.

"Aaaccckkk!" I screamed as the thick, black band sliced through my stomach and came out the other side.

I ran out of the bedroom pointing to his shoes and speaking in tongues: "Your shoes! Your-shoes-your-shoes-your-shoes!"

Then I told him, "I'm putting a cover on the couch."

"You are not," he told me. "I refuse to live in a house with furniture covers."

"Take off your shoes when you sit on the couch, then," I told him.

"I will not," he told me. "I refuse to live in a house where I have to take my shoes off to sit on my own couch."

I put a cover over the couch.

He took it off.

I put a cover over the couch.

He took it off.

Shoe polish formed its own arterial map through my consciousness before squeezing off the blood to my brain. I became vigilant, slinking around the house fixated on his feet. I hid behind a bookcase, watching. I ran out of the kitchen, hoping to catch him in the act. My days revolved around my daily examination of the couch skirt, the fruitless attempts to get the black out, the hopeless, helpless feeling when you finally have a decent crop of corn and locusts are coming.

I HAD MY monthly lunch at the Grange Hall with Ross and Charles.

"He's a slob," I said. "He's getting shoe polish on the couch. He won't get rid of his boxes. He throws his clothes all over and never picks them up."

"Oh? Did you marry him because he was a good house-keeper?" they asked.

AS LIFE AT home spiraled down, down, down, my most neurotic coping mechanisms kicked in. What would save the couch? Should I scream louder, move out, stick daggers in the goose down pillows? Should I yell, "Take off your shoes or I'm leaving you!" Is this what it comes to?

Right around that time, I finished and turned in my new book about relationships. It was called *How to Stay Lovers for Life: Discover a Marriage Counselor's Tricks of the Trade.* The book was all about marital generosity and giving your partner the benefit of the doubt. This led me to my next decision: that the only way I could get my husband to take care of the couch would be to buy him a new car. With a car that was spanking new and beautiful, he'd want to take care of it. He'd never had a new car in his life. (His old car had mice.) He couldn't *not* take care of it. A new car would fill him with pride. And he'd be so grateful. He'd *have* to take off his shoes when he sat on the couch.

The Dodge Caravan came out of the royalties for my book. I got him all the extras he wanted. There was money left over. Then, my husband went on tour to the Blue Note clubs in Osaka and Tokyo. The apartment was quiet. The couch didn't get dirtier. And, while he was thousands of miles away plucking the bass to "Round Midnight," an event occurred that simultaneously helped me grow up and put the final kibosh on the marriage.

I got a phone call from an old neighbor who'd moved out of our building five years earlier. Her brother worked in foreclosures at the bank, and he'd found her this incredible foreclosure in the West Village. When she had left our building, she had said, "If I ever find a great place for you through my brother, I'll call you." Now, after five years, she was telling me she'd seen something amazing.

"Buy it," she told me. "Buy it *immediately*. You will never find another place like this at this price. It has two floors and two entrances. You can see your patients downstairs. It's perfect for you. Call immediately before someone else grabs it."

Buying a place had never even crossed my mind. I'd just bought the car. It came to me that if he had a new car *and* a new house, he would feel great. And I could see my patients there, so I'd feel great, too. We might really be happy. Home might take on new meaning for us.

So I called, and the broker and owner met me in front of this hundred-year-old Greenwich Village brownstone, the kind that you walk by and wonder, "Who lives there?" It had previously been used for doctors' offices, and for some reason, after the foreclosure, the space had slipped through the cracks at the bank and remained empty for two years. It was one of the worst spaces on one of the best blocks in the village—a basement and a sub-basement with very little light. But I'd been a musician for many years and light mattered little to me. I preferred dark.

My friend told me that my next-door neighbor would be a supermodel. My upstairs neighbor would be the creative director of *Vogue*. Right across the street lived none other than Grace Paley.

I CALLED MY husband in Japan and said, "We bought a house."

He laughed.

Then, he came home and saw the paperwork.

NO MATTER WHAT he said about it, no matter what his concerns were, no matter how right or wrong they were, I refused to back down.

I wanted a safe place.

I wanted a home.

I wanted *this* home.

I wanted this home now!

We plowed ahead into a confusing world of mortgage rates and mortgage brokers and contractors and closings. It was as if all of a sudden, after fifty years on earth, I'd decided to grow up. All I wanted was for him to come with me to a better life.

I was absolutely sure he would.

IT WAS TWO weeks until moving day.

I was packing up stuff.

He told me not to touch his stuff. He'd pack his own stuff.

I was getting boxes from the liquor store.

I was only taking what was decent.

It was one week until moving day.

My husband had not packed a single thing.

"I'll get to it," he told me. "When the day comes, I'll be ready."

It was two days until moving day.

My husband had not packed one single thing.

"I'm going to pull an all-nighter. Believe me, I've done

this before. I'll get home from my gig and stay up all night. You have nothing to worry about."

It was one day until moving day.

He didn't even have empty boxes.

"I know what I'm doing," he said.

On the morning of moving day, I found him sprawled on the couch—nothing packed.

I moved without him.

HE ARRIVED WEEKS later, towing his torn, moldy boxes and his greasy paper bags. He piled these injured containers in the living room so we could hardly walk through it.

But by then I had already managed to transform my downstairs consultation room into something I'd never had before—anywhere, ever.

I WANT TO tell you about decorating my one safe place, the office where I see my patients. I began by collecting the things I deeply love—therapeutic things. A seventy-million-year-old chunk of oyster bed, a memento from my geologist friend's Calgary farm, perches on a birch bookcase built for me by an artist whose carpentry I love. There is no ocean in Calgary today, and the oyster bed reminds me to delve beyond what I can see—deeper to the underground waters. An antique French dental cabinet reminds me that therapy can be like pulling teeth. Three jars of seashells from my best friend Karen's beach ensure that no one ever feels land-locked. Mary Jones's oil painting is like a mood ring for my patients (Danny loves it, Loralee hates it, Suzannah checks to see if it matches her clothes, Alf sees the sun in the upper left-hand corner while his wife, Janet, sees a monster in the same place). An African mud cloth from my friend Bangally which displays my love of African art. The white sage and sweetgrass from the Native American store around the corner help to call up ancestors who meet the require-ments for emotional archeological digs and to get rid of bad karma. In case of a medical emergency, there is a first aid kit. In case of a flood, a pair of oars.

How important is the therapy room to the patient? Studies suggest which therapy *styles* work best, but are there studies on which therapy *rooms* work best?

Many psychotherapists work best in a spare room. In fact, many therapists prefer to let patients bring their own furniture. For example, a patient might carry in a child-hood bureau painted pale blue with horses; luggage that won't fit under the seat; a large, green banister to slide down; the kitchen table where he or she got spankings; or an Oldsmobile with automatic windows that choked a three-year-old sister.

As for me, I need to feel safe in order to make my patients feel safe. I am not like some lucky others who carry their safe place inside them. I'm the one waiting to be pushed off the subway platform into an oncoming train. I am the one waiting for the car to careen onto the sidewalk and hit me. It's a big job to make this twelve-by-twelve-foot container strong enough to hold me—*and* hold Danny's horrible family, *and* hold Anita's second miscarriage and the way her husband wept over the empty crib, *and* hold Eve's abusive father and her father's abusive father. Echoes of an Edward Albee play are a shoe-polish stain away.

Many suggest that a job like mine, listening to other people's problems all day long, would make them crazy. Therapists have common responses for such probes: "It is my privilege to hear my patient's inner thoughts." "I am a trained professional, so it isn't the same for me as it would be for you." "I go away for the month of August every year, and that gives me time to recoup." I, on the other hand, can hold all my patients and myself because, as Eve reminded me, these traumas are where I live, where I have *always* lived.

At four years of age, I was watching *The Florence Nightingale Story* with my grandmother. I ran into the kitchen and started collecting rags to help the soldiers. I started wrapping fake broken arms. I spent weeks considering how much whiskey to give an injured patient before amputating a leg. I thoughtfully examined my family's scabs, and, without being able to pronounce the word, I learned the point of a tourniquet.

Years later, I set up a table in the garage where I pretended to operate on Steven Omartian, our next-door neighbor. I removed his heart with a barbecue fork. I placed his kidneys side by side in a shoebox and gave him better ones—made from candy corn. In second grade, my classmate Cynthia had a brain tumor removed. I went to the hospital to see the hole in her head. I took a picture. I put the potty under her and emptied it out. In high school, I visited my mother's friend with bedsores. Her husband was always out of town.

At home, as chief surgeon of the bird hospital and the toad rest home in my backyard, I learned all there was to know about broken bodies and eye-drop feedings. I never minded blood and guts, except when it came to events that occurred when I was eleven.

That year (the year that looked the same upside down: 1961) marked the beginning of my grandmother's suicide. It started one day when my grandfather was doing his favorite thing: watching a ball game with one hand holding a cigar and the other on the control panel of his old, brown La-Z-Boy. My grandmother had recently fallen in a supermarket and broken her back. She was confined to her bed. It was hours later, after the ball game ended, after he did not respond to her calls, when she called a friend to come over. My grandfather was dead. He'd had a heart attack before the final inning.

I was sent to stay with my grandmother. It was my job to cheer her up.

We slept in the bed she'd shared with my grandfather.

From midnight to four in the morning, she'd moan and scream and beg to die.

When she came home from shock therapy, she drooled all over our pillows.

Once her back healed, she spent her days tying nooses and storing Seconal.

I was in sixth grade.

One day after school, I went to the cellar to do the laundry and found her standing on a chair with a rope thrown over a beam. I walked past her and put in a load of whites. I never mentioned it to anyone. Soon, the whole family moved into my grandmother's house, and although my grandmother's behavior continued on a regular basis, no one mentioned it.

I went to my new school every day, trying to adjust to the new kids, and came home to the grandmother who continued to string her suicide out for more than a year. It was my job to stop her.

Eventually, in spite of her moans, I would doze off. Then, in my dreams, spiders fell out of me, tumbled to the ground, and scurried around the house. Small buzzards shot from my eyes, bouncing off walls like cartoon critters. In the mornings, my sisters walked out of their room, and I imagined them shaking buzzards from their hair. I was sure they eyed me with suspicion.

MY GRANDMOTHER DID not get better. I could hear my father and mother fighting over what to do about her.

"Do something."

"She's your mother. You do something."

Fix-ups with old men, red hair dye, department store makeovers, visits to Florida, shock therapy—nothing helped. So she went into a nursing home that threw her out when she pulled the noose bit on them.

It is strange to see your grandmother naked on a bed, nipples brushing her belly, frail as a cornflake. "Rub my feet, will you?" "Make a little tea, will you?" It is strange that you rub her feet again and again, that you make the tea, that she hangs herself anyway. It is strange that she hangs herself just days after she baked you your special rice pudding with extra raisins.

My parents did not let me go to the funeral because I murdered her.

And I'm not the only one to blame myself.

ALLIE SITS IN my office looking at her hands as she tells me, "I came home from school, and I found my mother in the bathtub with two long vertical slits on her wrists. I fainted, and I was out for almost thirty minutes. I know that my mother was alive when I found her. If I hadn't fainted, she'd be alive. Do you understand? She *planned* for me to save her life." Allie has never told her husband how her mother died, and she lives in fear of being found out.

Roberta's mom wrote a good-bye letter to all the kids after a bad face-lift. She said she was killing herself because she could no longer close her eyes. Roberta tells me, "That's what the note said, but she was just trying to protect me. I was such a difficult child for her. I caused her so much pain."

Dave's dad put a gun to his head and shot himself twice. Dave and I have spent three years talking about that second shot. "What went through his mind after that first shot? Was he still alive? Was he too embarrassed to live?"

Every suicide is a homicide.

We missed the signs, ignored the pills, loaded the guns, pushed loved ones out the open windows, prayed it would end soon, looked the other way.

And we got away with it.

The authorities didn't come.

We still got into college, married, started families.

When swallowed, guilt is reconfigured. Allie makes her toddlers take showers instead of baths. They stand crying in the stall. Roberta counts the remaining Valium in her bottle and wonders if it is enough. Dave cannot move on with his life until he figures out the second shot and how his father did it.

We sit in my new office like big lumps.

From time to time, on days when I am a little tired or stressed, I find myself blinking once, blinking twice—convinced I see my patients pulling little buzzards out of their hair, just as I thought my sisters did so many years ago. This dream has stuck with me. I have it over and over and over again.

Since I am prone to seeing buzzards, I burn sage to keep them away. Since I am prone to drowning, I like to know the oars are there. I keep my office safe. Don't kid yourself and think I'm overdoing it. My patients have been raped by brothers, priests, middle-aged women in their mothers' mah-jongg clubs. I see a young man who grew up in the back of a van drinking out of a Johnnie Walker Black bottle. I sit as calmly with these patients as I did with one man I will tell you about later—a man who fucked his daughter and handed me a Milky Way.

Fathers beat sons. Fathers beat mothers. Mothers don't leave. Relatives don't notice. Families flock around the tormentors to keep them safe, the tormented to keep them quiet. Amputations can heal much faster with a swig of corn liquor. I know this. It's an old scrapbook for me, a bouncing ball of childhood. My patients can't make me sad, because I am already sad. I'm not the kind of person you can make jump out of her skin. I remember when I saw *Shoah*. In one interview with an Israeli general-cum-concentration camp survivor, he said, "If you lick my heart, it would poison you."

Upstairs, I imagine black streaks of shoe polish are winding around the banister, across the microwave, and through the bathtub of our new home. Upstairs, boxes and trash are appearing instead of disappearing. Upstairs, every time I scrub the shoe polish I only make it worse. But it doesn't matter.

Because downstairs I am cradled by secret oceans, ancient oyster beds, feathers, and vanilla scents. Waves lap my feet as I watch the drama of my baby sea turtles digging their way out of deep holes and scuttling to the sea. If they take a wrong turn here or there, I lend a helping hand. I know they will make it. They come and go, come and go. When my office is an empty shell, it means that somebody's left my safe home because they have found their safe home. Soon, someone else will find a safe home with me. There is room for us all.

Need a place to cry?

Need an amputation?

Need a lifeboat?

•　　•　　•

why I stayed married: **reason #7**

WE CLIMBED THE towers of La Sagrada Familia and sat with the albino gorilla in Barcelona. We took a train ride from Barcelona to Paris with our own personal butler. We got soaked to our knees in rainy Venice because the city flooded and our cheap hotel was not near the planks they set down in the nicer parts of town. And we found our little spot in Paris with the aid of a Frommer's guide. The elevator could only hold one person with no suitcases, so my husband carried our bags up to the third floor. The guide said the hotel was spotless and under the watchful eye of Mademoiselle Gabon. I looked under the bed in our room and found four pink hair rollers. My husband kept looking and calling out for Mademoiselle Gabon—"*Mademoiselle Gabon, Mademoiselle Gabon, ou est vouz* and your special touch?" He got teary over the Mozart in the music room at the British Museum, and we both got teary over the naturally mummified young man who fell between two glaciers thousands of years ago. His prehistoric tools showed he had been hunting, and we imagined he was on his way home to his wife and children. We rafted in Montana and counted beaver. We drank glacier waters in Banff. We knelt by the Anasazi Indian ruins in Arizona. We climbed the Dolomites, yodeling badly.

For my birthday one year, I told my husband that I wanted to outdo our trip the year before, when we'd gone to see the Gaudi sites in Barcelona. This did not seem possible to outdo, but he said he'd give it some thought.

We spent the night before my birthday in Trieste, in a grand marble hotel overlooking a piazza in the center of town. It was nice, I thought to myself, but it was no Sagrada Familia.

The next morning, it was pouring.

He told me to dress warmly and bring stuff for a whole day out. We got in the car, and we drove to the border of what had been Yugoslavia. The sign was torn down and painted across. He had a story prepared for the border patrol agents because we needed a visa, even for a day visit. He said we were going to a resort in Puma that was still open.

We drove our tiny Fiat through the militarized borders. We passed slowly through Croatia, where we stopped frequently, keeping to our tale. We bought some Croatian money. We drove along the Adriatic. We passed torn-down signs, evacuated cities, graffiti-covered banks. We drove into the mountains where we found a city that appeared to have erupted organically out of the brown mountain on which it sat. It probably hadn't changed in the past five hundred years.

We stopped for pizza in Slovenia. We sat quietly, on my birthday, chewing pizza and looking out a window at graffiti-covered signs and empty streets. I never imagined we'd take such a risk. We weren't like that. We hiked on designated trails. We obeyed all the rules. But this year, because of my husband, we broke all the rules, and it was thrilling. Our hearts pounded every minute we were on Slovenian soil.

We gave the waitress all the money we'd changed for her tip.

chapter 8

When Will the Children Be Safe?

We did not speak of my grandmother as my family took the reins of the house where both she and my mother had grown up and where my great-grandparents had lived since the early 1900s. What we did instead was have never-ending tag sales—tag sales to erase all signs of what and who went before. Because, now that my grandmother was gone, we were all moving into this family house for good. Nothing was too insignificant for a price tag—from the old empty borscht jars to 1920s extra-length bobby pins to the pineapple lamp my Aunt Irene brought back from her Wac days in Hawaii to warped Molly Picon 78 rpm records to a tin of anchovies from the old country. My great-great-grandmother's horsehair wig sold for ten cents. A broken crystal set sold for a quarter. We tagged four generations of our family and watched ourselves disappear from sight.

The highlight was the sale of the immense ebony Steinway grand piano that had dominated the living room, untouched and untuned, for almost as long as the house had been there. My sisters and I stood like the three little "see no evil, hear no evil, speak no evil" monkeys as the moving men lifted the hulking Steinway and all four of the piano legs fell off onto the floor. The surprised movers almost lost their grip, and we shrieked in amazement, trailing behind them as they clumsily maneuvered our legless piano down the front porch stairs.

We sold the aluminum ashtray in the shape of an upturned hand, into which my grandfather had flicked his smelly cigar on the day he died. We sold the dilapidated African violets that my grandmother had once pruned endlessly. We sold the kosher and non-kosher sets of dishes in the cupboards.

One of the last things to go was the meat grinder that had long been a permanent fixture in the big pantry. My great-grandfather had been a kosher butcher. I remember, when I was young, we ground all our meat ourselves. I even remember going to his butcher store when I was three. He said, "Dis lem chop is for you," and he handed me a brown paper wrapper. I refused to let go of my special lamb chop until it went into a frying pan.

Also standing in the pantry, but not for sale, was a three-foot-high bottle of Haig & Haig whiskey that my father won in a raffle but never drank. Through my preteen and teen years, I would remove the alcohol bit by bit, drinking it and replacing it with water. This process, which began in 1961, was not discovered until late 1967, when my father's boss, a whiskey drinker, came over for dinner. (Years later, I discovered that one of my sisters had been doing the exact same thing.)

Finally, everything in our soon-to-be new house was emptied out, and we packed up our little old house. We put the living room furniture from our old house in the den where my grandfather died. We'd been previously squeezed into a post-World War II ticky-tacky box, and now we luxuriated in a thirteen-room colonial with window boxes. Our old living room furniture barely took up half of the den in our new house. We had no furniture to replace what we'd sold. For years, the living room lay bare except for a card table and red folding chairs. This made my house very popular with friends, because we could run everywhere inside without breaking anything and because it was so unusual—everyone else had furniture. At one point, I won a nickel bet with a kid who could not believe we didn't have furniture.

I was moved from my grandmother's bedroom into my Uncle Sheldon's old bedroom, where his old bookcase was still filled with FBI books. There, I pondered photos of Lucky Luciano on a slab in the morgue. I went on to become a quasi-expert on Jewish gangsters, recognizing not only their photos but also the photos of their finger-prints. I contemplated my future as a G-man.

In this neighborhood, there were doctors and lawyers instead of Jif peanut butter salesmen and soda deliverymen. There was not a single fireman or piece worker to be found. The state representative who lived next door had the first color television we ever saw. Sometimes I would sit at the window of my room and watch his daughters, who were the same ages as my sisters and me. They wore ensemble sweater sets of lustrous aqua mohair and cherry loafers, always new. Their hair was straight and thick and shiny, and it never frizzed. These girls performed marvelous feats, such as going to Florida on vacations, appearing fresh and unrumpled on even the hottest days, and always being chosen first. The mother, wearing a year-round tan and a tennis bracelet, chain-smoked and woke up elegant every single day.

My mother had her work cut out. She began to madly sew us all new clothes so we could keep up appearances. Her mistake was that she would sew many of our dresses out of the same material. Some days, all of us arrived at the breakfast table in matching yellow-and-purple-striped A-line dresses.

My mother was a big splash here. The very same yellow and purple that made me look like a consumptive zebra made her look swell. I always knew she was beautiful, but she became much more beautiful in this neighborhood, where the men seemed more confident.

Everywhere we went (without my father), men complimented her. "Gorgeous," said the butcher, who gave her free meat. "Electric," said the hardware store clerk, who discounted the light bulbs. It was tough work being eleven and making the rounds with a mother who looked liked this, a mother who was thirty. I remember the day Mrs. Solomon and Mrs. Marshall had their thick legs up on their lawn chairs, nylons rolled down, and were arguing. "She looks like Debbie Reynolds. They're twins," Mrs. Solomon said while she sucked a chicken bone. "No, you're wrong," Mrs. Marshall insisted through a mouthful of coleslaw. "Pretend her hair is black. If her hair were black, she'd look like Liz Taylor."

I adopted her hairstyle, sneaked her Maybelline products, studied the delicate operation of her eyelashes, fought to keep my pigeon toes pointed straight, and, as she instructed me, tucked my tummy in when I walked. It was so much to remember, and it didn't work for me anyway. I'd peek through her bedroom door, trying to fold into the *whoosh* of her white slip as she slipped it over her remarkable blue-eyed, blonde head. I grabbed my throat and wished for a fat mother in a grape juice-stained housedress.

WITH MY GRANDMOTHER gone, I toyed with the hope of a fresh start as a G-man with other G-men friends. This was not to be. My parents began to host weekly bridge games with you-know-who and his wife. I'd had a welcome reprieve from him while living with my grandmother, but that was over now. The four of them played cards downstairs in the kitchen. There was a little bathroom right there. But on most Tuesday nights, my father's best friend came up the stairs to where I slept.

No one asked, "Hey, why were you gone so long?"

Or said, "Geez, there's a toilet three feet away. Use that."

TUESDAY.

I slept with my clothes on—socks, too.

Tuesday.

I went to other places, great white spaces where it was warm.

Tuesday.

I added extra blankets to my bed to make myself harder to find.

Tuesday.

Fanged bugs gnawed me from the inside out.

A couple of years of Tuesdays.

Six days are days before.

Six days are days after.

Finally, one Tuesday night, after he'd walked out of my room and into the bathroom, I found something between the buzzards and the blankets—a voice. I jumped out of bed, ran to the banister, leaned over, and yelled like a Jewish gangster, "Come here! Come here!"

My parents ran to the bottom of the steps. Because of

the overhang, I could only see them from the waist down. I called down the steps, "I want a lock on my bedroom door right now. He's coming in my room."

Silence.

So I said it again, and my father's head seemed to click, as if he were really an alien inside. His voice rose in a way that was scarier than his friend's advances, scarier than the way he was one night when he could not stop spanking me, scarier than Alfred Hitchcock's *Lifeboat*.

It's not that my father never yelled, but I never heard him yell like that. His voice was more than a yell—it was the curdling, choking, high-pitched screech of a bull on the wrong end of the castration line.

I saw my mother's feet step back.

"Damn it! Get in your room and shut up!" he yelled. He kept yelling the same thing again and again.

Then the bathroom door opened, and his friend walked out.

They all went back to the card game.

FRAN DID NOT cry last year in my office when she told me that her three-year-old sister was raped by their two brothers. Fran was six and spent hours in therapy wondering if she was stronger than her brothers. She thinks, but she has never been sure, that she may have been strong enough to fight them off. One day, her mother and her aunt came home while the brothers had the little sister pinned and Fran was trying to punch them. Fran's mother screamed, "You girls stop it! Don't punch your brothers like that!" Fran and her sister got so scared that they ran under the bed and stayed there—all night. Fran has not been able to like a penis since.

Hallie was twelve when her father brushed by her in the kitchen in *that* way. At a recent family reunion, she discovered he'd brushed by her cousins in *that* way, too.

When Rudy was ten, he told his family doctor, "My mother touches me here." He was trying to tell the doctor that his mother was masturbating him. The doctor said, "All mothers do."

Natalie was fourteen when her math teacher raped her. "He made me give him oral sex every day until I graduated."

Can it be true that so many adults are working overtime to ignore what is going on? How can they find so many ways to believe that nothing horrible is happening to their children?

AFTER THE NIGHT on the stairs, my dad did not look at me. Once, when he had to give me a ride to the beach two hours away, not a word passed between us on the trip. Sometimes, though, I noticed him watching me. When I was out with friends, he would pop up. If I was at a friend's house, the phone would ring, but there would be no one on the line. I knew it was him.

Why did he call?

Why did he hang up?

Why was he following me?

Why did he offer me up to his friend?

It was because of the night on the stairs—the night of my innocent penetration into his unspeakable core.

My father, my father, my tall, handsome father who did amazing card tricks and always had a funny story to tell. My father who dressed in full drag for the community center show and sang "A Good Man Is Hard to Find." My father who made all my babysitters swoon and clutch their hearts. My father who was the pitcher for the local softball team (they called him Clarabelle because he was such a clown) till the day he died. My father who played all the Frank Sinatra roles in all the Neil Simon plays at the local community center. My father who modeled for a department store and was in a television commercial. My father who played the tenor guitar and sang "Artificial Flowers," sounding just like Bobby Darin. My father with biceps the size of coconuts. My father who played golf for the first time in his life and won the tournament.

My father with the horrible best friend. My father who gambled with the grocery money. My father who had his little girls lie to the bookies on the phone that we were sick and he wasn't home. My father who thought it funny to have his six-year-old daughter place his bets. My father who thought it was a riot that he walked around the house naked and semi-erect. My father who lay in bed with us watching television and scratching his balls. My father who forged my mother's signature on IOUs, who pissed away all of our inheritances, who likely received stolen goods from the Brink's robbery and who would have gone to jail a year later—like his best friend—if he hadn't died instead.

More than twenty years later, I got a phone call that helped me understand why he couldn't look at me yet couldn't leave me alone.

A YEAR OR so ago, my father's sister and I had our annual holiday chat. After years of maintaining the Pollyanna version of life, my aunt, to my surprise, said, "I'm on Prozac. I've been depressed all my life." And she began to tell me about her real childhood, the one I'd never heard about before.

"My parents owned a little diner. They worked fifteen-hour days, seven days a week. They kept the cash in a safe in the house. They never used a bank. There was a lady my mother hired to take care of us—dad, your Uncle Sammy, and me. She was there when the three of us came home from school.

"As soon as I walked in the door, she locked me in the bathroom. I wasn't allowed to come out till she let me. Then she took your dad, he was ten, and Sammy, he was twelve, into their bedroom and had sex with both of them. They told me. Anyway, I could hear them.

"When I told my mother about being locked in the bathroom, you know what she said? She said, 'I need her. Try to make do.'"

NOW I KNOW that when I yelled "Come here!" I strapped my father into a time machine. He landed in his bedroom with his cock in the hired lady while his brother sucked her tits and his little sister cried in the bathroom.

What could he do but blow up when he found out about me?

He felt as helpless as he'd felt when it was happening to him.

So he followed me around but never said or did a thing.

Does knowing this help me in any way?

Does it offer relief?

Does it make me feel compassion or forgiveness for my confused, abused father? No, no, and no.

He used me.

After the night when my father screamed, the dream spiders did a West Side Story rumble in my chest. I lay in my room and imagined that the towels in our bathroom were from Israel and that they were all dead. Suddenly, as I write this, it finally makes sense—little concentration camp prisoners lined the walls. I sat at the kitchen table and turned bowls of ice cream over on top of my head. I swallowed bottles of pills. An usher removed me from a Jerry Lewis movie because I was crying so hard.

Nothing brought relief from the blacksmith of my body, from the gas and debris that twisted and clanged.

When my parents went to the movies, I went into the bathroom, ignoring the dead prisoners who lined the walls. I took a razor blade and began slicing my thighs. It tickled, as I knew it would. I kept going and a giggle slipped out. I could not use the dead towels, so blood dripped down my legs. Looking for a sting, I poured a bottle of alcohol over my legs, but I didn't even feel it. After countless slices, the spiders and the gas had an exit and the pressure inside eased up.

How can I explain this little pleasure of drawing blood? Standing in the bathroom like a building contractor, I tried to design one long slice from the middle of the top of my head down the middle of my face and the middle of my body through my clitoris and up and around the other side. Then, everything inside me could get out. Then, I realized, everything outside me could also get in.

This was in 1963.

Today, journals are filled with articles about teenagers who perform what the books call "self-mutilation." Conferences are offered where therapists can learn all about it. When I recently tried to read a big story on the topic in one of the magazines, I couldn't even get past the first sentence. I cannot bear the way the experts and journalists write about it—the clinical, detached labels, diagnoses, treatment plans, outcomes.

Here's what I think:

The holes in our bodies don't work.

Our mouths don't work, so nothing will come out of them.

The holes in our noses for breathing are useless.

Our anuses stay covered if we are lucky.

Our vaginas are holes where things go in, not out.

How are we supposed to get some relief?

Cutters are simply and elegantly trying to make more holes in order to get the poisons out. Thus, my job as a therapist is to help my patients make better use of the holes they already have so they don't have to make new ones—even if making new holes feels so damn good.

Current literature regarding children who have been sexually abused suggests that the kind of support the child is offered when he or she finally tells someone has a direct correlation to the depth of the scars.

That night, dripping red streamers, I paraded naked into my little sisters' room. They were in bed but not sleeping. "Look, look, look at me," I said. I had my hands up in the air, as I executed a perfect pirouette. "That's ketchup," one concluded.

I laughed and I laughed and I laughed and I laughed my way right into a psychiatric hospital.

This is the intergenerational fiasco I bring to my profession and my marriage. Why, as a therapist, does this prove functional, even healing, when, as a wife, it feels like a continuation of the same?

EMBARRASSED BY MY sudden relocation to the other side of town, my mother told my school and our neighbors that I had stomach problems. This worked for a day or so, but the hospital insisted that I go to school every day of my three-month stay. Thus, I was back in my homeroom, coming and going on a different bus and at a loss to explain what exactly was wrong with my stomach.

While I was in the hospital, I met the mother of a boy I knew who'd left a noose on my classroom desk. She'd slit her own throat and walked around with her neck swathed in gauze. When he came to visit her one night and saw me, he started to cry.

Did this make me feel sorry for him?

Did this make me like him better?

Did I care that now I understood him?

No, no, and no.

He humiliated me, and I hated him.

Another woman had swallowed small pieces of a vacuum cleaner that clogged up her intestines. Large doses of laxatives were not budging Her Hooverness, so she finally had to be vacuumed out her own backside. She gave us all the details. My neighbor banged his head against the wall of his room that was right next to my bed. At breakfast, we'd try not to notice the big green-black-and-blue scabs that sat on top of the big green-and-yellow scabs. One woman swore up and down that Dean Martin loved her and was coming to get her. We helped her put on full makeup and pack her bag every night and unpack it every morning as she sobbed through her raccoon eyes. She shared a room with the lady who did not believe in washing her cream rinse out of her hair. "Why put it in if you're going to wash it out?" she'd say as her oily, stringy curls plastered themselves to her face like sea kelp.

One man (whom I mentioned earlier) had sex with his daughter, but he called it "diddling." Even when I heard this, in the middle of group therapy, while all the other birds screeched and beat their wings, I sat calmly. That night, he brought candy bars for all the girls, but I was the only girl to take one. I could not bear the pleading look in his eyes as he held the Milky Way out to me.

My roommate, Shirley, was the saddest case of all. She said, "I'm seventy. Do you know that no one has touched me in forty years? Only a doctor to take my pulse. I haven't been hugged by man, woman, or child."

I loved these people. I chose a husband who would have fit right into the group.

THREE MONTHS LATER, I came home, having never told anyone in the hospital what happened to me in my house. I was now fourteen.

The first night I came home from the psychiatric hospital, my father came into my bedroom as I was lying in the dark. He climbed into my bed and put his arms around me. He kissed me once on the neck before he caught a whiff of the afterbirth of my abuse. I smelled molested. He got up and left.

My father never told. His silence tortured him into using me.

I never told, but I would never use children.

So, even though I would have been a wonderful mother, I didn't have any children.

I want credit for that.

·   ·   ·

why I stayed married: reason #8

DURING LABOR DAY weekend, I woke up in the middle of the night with a raging headache—the kind where you know something is very wrong. My husband hustled me to the emergency room at Beth Israel Hospital, a place you don't want to be when you have the world's worst HMO, which, as a graduate student, I did. I spent seventeen hours on a stretcher in the hall—like you see in a television drama. I couldn't get a doctor to look at me.

Finally, an inept and cocky first-year resident gave me a spinal tap, and they admitted me with viral meningitis. I was placed in a scummy four-bed ward. One woman was on oxygen—while, a few feet away, another woman was smoking crack with her boyfriend. The fourth woman had Alzheimer's; she was ranting and kicking, and had to be restrained. Too sick to protest my lousy digs, I lay there in a Demerol stupor, puking sloppily. I demanded the Demerol every four hours as much to drown out my surroundings as to alleviate the pain.

Later that night, Alzheimer's lady was carted off and replaced by a woman rescued from a welfare nursing home. She was covered with bedsores that went all the way to the bone. Though I could be having nightmares to this day about crack-lady blowing up the room because of oxygen-lady, it is the bedsores that cling.

My husband came every day with my favorite treats. He fed me. He grinned ear to ear as I chewed a grilled cheese sandwich. He walked me down the hall, balancing my IV. "You look like a baby flamingo," he told me, "only cuter." I knew that if I lost my arms or my legs or my breasts, he wouldn't flinch.

Whenever we went on holiday, I would buy all the trash-iest magazines—the silliest I could find—and read every one with gusto. He said I was wasting our money. He said he would never read something so stupid.

Then, one morning, he appeared with a copy of the *Weekly World News*, my trashiest favorite. It seemed that the captain of the Titanic had been found floating in a dinghy in the middle of the ocean—sitting straight up, his cigar still lit. My husband proceeded to read me the whole damn paper.

"Because of weather conditions, his body had not dete-riorated one bit."

chapter 9

Therapy, Therapy, Therapy

*P*erhaps by now you are thinking that I should be in therapy. I am, and I have been for years, since long before we moved into our brownstone. My therapist's name is Lucy. Lucy is also in therapy. Her therapist's name is Sam. We are a long line of therapists screwed to the therapy chain. Lucy is one rung up from me. Sam is at the top of the chain, next to the clasp. If Sam needs a therapist, he has to suck it up or talk to his wife. I guess that's what they mean when they say it's lonely at the top.

Lucy is perfect for me, even though she ruined my life. Here's why: When I met her so long ago, I was renting the smelly Chinese food office. I mentioned it during our second session, and she actually said something. If you have been in therapy, you know what I mean when I say how rare is to have your therapist actually make a direct, concrete statement that suggests a direct, concrete action that might actually help you.

"You don't belong there," she said with utter conviction. "You're a 'downtown therapist.' I know someone who has a new suite with an office she's looking to rent. I'll call her for you to see if it's still available. Then you can call her and use my name."

A month later, I moved into a beautiful office that I got to paint and decorate myself. I was so much happier that I immediately began to make more money.

When I met Lucy, I lived with my husband in that crowded crash pad with boxes surrounding the white couch with the black racing stripe on the skirt. She lived in her wonderful downtown loft with her wonderful downtown office as part of it. As our sessions passed, my loft lust grew exponentially. Instead of killing her off and taking her stuff, the good therapy she gave me helped me conquer my envy and come to desire my own house with my own office as part of it. My good therapy took me to the point where I could do more than fantasize: I could make a down payment. And I did.

When I moved downtown, Lucy continued to help me. She gave me the numbers of the secret leftist window-blind man who only measured blinds for the politically aware. She called and cancelled my appointment with the electrician I didn't like when I was too afraid to call him myself. She was . . . actually . . . nice to me.

Lucy gave me the idea that I might actually be nicer to my own patients, too. That's how I started getting more patients.

Just by being as nice to them as Lucy was to me.

This was an option I hadn't learned anything about in therapy school.

When I got the right therapist and the right office and the right house and the right way to handle envy, I discovered that I had the wrong husband—like those what-doesn't-fit pictures in *Children's Digest*. When I had the wrong house and the wrong office, the wrong husband didn't stick out like a sore thumb. I even thought I was happily married, more or less. This should not be hard to explain. I was happier than I was in my Uncle Sheldon's room. I was happier than I was when I was in the hospital. I was happier than I was with my former husbands. If happiness is a comparative study, I was happy in spite of the couch.

I assumed that what was wrong with my life was wrong inside of me.

I find that my patients also assume that what is wrong with their lives is wrong with them. I work with them to help them see that what is wrong inside of them is their difficulty seeing what they are doing to themselves, and then doing something about it. The therapeutic community has all kinds of phrases for this that aren't worth going into here.

Lucy ruins my life by wanting as much for me as she wants for herself. She ruins my life with love. She asks my permission to ruin it. She never takes advantage. She never says something just to sound smart—a common therapist downfall, of which I was guilty before I met her. "I made a mistake," she freely admits when she makes a mistake. I wasn't used to this—therapy with someone who would actually help me get better.

Still, you must understand—if you understand nothing else in this whole book: *Every therapist will ruin your life. Find one who ruins it for the better.*

Most therapists will just about force you to revisit painful aspects of your life, creepy parts of yourself, and the disappointing if not dreadful behavior of your family, in order to help you make sense of the mess you are in now. A bad therapist ruins your life by not knowing how to shepherd you through this drama safely. A good therapist ruins your life by guiding you to changes you never thought you'd have to make in the first place. Sure, with a good therapist you get "better," but "better" doesn't mean "easy."

I am an expert at being ruined and at ruining. I had a long psychiatric career before I met Lucy, meaning I'd been to—or, possibly, through—many therapists in the past. I used to keep a list of therapists the way some girls keep a list of the guys they've slept with. I have bared my body to my share of men, but the list of therapists I've bared my soul to is longer. If I count my previous therapists, the number would be around twenty-nine. This does not include the occasional drive-by sessions, the therapy equivalent of one-night stands. I've had almost every kind of therapist and therapy there is. As I think back, I get scared to think that a patient could walk into an office and end up with some of the dorks I've ended up with.

There was the beautiful English psychologist, Susan, who developed a crush on a close friend of mine and called me up to ask me if I minded if she fucked him. Soon after, she invited me to breakfast so she could mine my knowledge of him. When he dumped her, I was her first call.

There was the psychiatrist who wore white pants without having properly wiped his ass after taking a shit. I had trouble taking prescriptions from him.

There was the one who told me I was faking and insisted I leave his office. Why would you fake unhappiness? And, isn't faking unhappiness sick?

There was the short cigar-smoking, Cadillac-driving psychiatrist from the psychiatric hospital who took me on a five-hour drive to view the Indian mystic and avatar Meher Baba's shoes.

I remember asking him, "What would Meher Baba say about you owning a fancy Cadillac?"

"Meher Baba would say, 'prosper and enjoy,'" he replied, as I began to notice how much he and Meher resembled each other.

When we arrived at the house of the Baba acolytes who were the keepers of the shoes, and as I walked slowly in the long line of people who had driven hundreds of miles to pass by a glass case that held slippers, I began to wonder which one of us should be locked up.

Back in those days, most of my therapists were a bunch of wacky-wacks. I didn't think anything, except screwing my best friend, was too strange or out of bounds for a therapist to say or do.

I made it very easy to be my therapist.

These days, it is very hard to be my therapist because all the therapy phrases that my therapist learned in school, I learned in school, too. If Lucy uses one that would have worked great on me twenty years ago, I can tell her which textbook page it was on. In fact, I do. And no matter how many times she asks me, no matter how tired or sad or troubled I am, I WILL NOT LIE DOWN ON THE COUCH FOR HER. NOR WILL I CRY. I WILL NOT GIVE HER THE SATISFACTION.

As I say this, I have a sudden memory of another time I would not give the satisfaction. I was seven, and I was bad. My father came into my bedroom to spank me. I had been waiting there until he came home. I had been thinking about the spanking to come, imagining it over and over again. When he finally arrived, when the anticipation of his arrival was no longer, when he finally spanked me—I laughed. I don't know why it tickled so exquisitely, but it did. When he spanked me harder, I laughed harder. "Damn it!" he screamed, as his face changed from obligation to rage. Suddenly, he got a choke hold on my fanny, and began to slap the bejesus out of it. The harder he spanked, the louder I laughed, the madder he got, the harder he spanked, the louder I laughed.

He had never paid so much attention to me in my entire life.

Drawing this kind of connection is what therapy is made of. It takes me from being a smart-ass to being very sad. In fact, as I write this chapter, I am giving myself therapy because I am making this connection right now, going through the sadness right now. I am wondering if this is the first time I've made such a connection between pain and pleasure. I am wondering if I came to seek out this intimate pleasure over and over again throughout my life, in one way or another.

Of course, I was already sad when I woke up today. I haven't been able to write for weeks. I think about what Lucy would say to me if she were here. She would ask me what feeling I have, and she would suggest that maybe I should be writing about that. I've seen Lucy for long enough that I can take her with me into my writing office. I see her because I love her. And she has told me that she loves me.

When I think of my father spanking me and of myself laughing louder and louder, I realize that not much has changed. Life spanks me. I laugh louder. (What begins as defiance ends as hysteria.) So now I know this—I make yet another connection.

Does knowing this help me feel better?

IN MY OFFICE, Colette reads a letter she wrote and will never mail to her present and past bad boyfriends: "I have never been anyone's priority. I am no one's special person, no one's soul mate, no one's deep love. I have never been the one you think about before you fall asleep or when you see a pretty bouquet of flowers. No one waits for my phone call or thrills to the sound of my voice. No one has ever thought that they can't live without me."

She dissolves into a torrent of hugely cathartic tears.

But has she dumped her present bad boyfriend?

Later that day, Timmy says, "I am a fetus. You are attempting to do therapy with the unborn."

Timmy has never kissed a girl. Never a hot date or a sweet fuck. Before therapy, he figured it was hopeless. He asked me to put him on an iceberg with the ancient Inuits and banish him to the icy sea.

Now, after years of therapy, he has hope.

But does he have a girlfriend?

I HAVE DECIDED to try to end my marriage while my husband tries not to end his. I try to get strong enough to call a lawyer and strong enough to suggest to my husband that we should see a divorce mediator. Trying to get stronger makes me feel worse every day. I miss the husband with whom I've only eaten dinner three times in the past two years. I miss cuddling with him. We haven't slept in the same bed for two years. I miss his dry wit. He hasn't used it with me in two years. I miss the great vacations. I miss when I thought I was happy, and when I thought all the problems were inside of me. Especially, I miss the fantasy that when I understood my spankings and agreed not to let myself be spanked by hand or deed, I'd be happy. Yes, that's it:

What I miss most is being fucked up.

I go to Lucy. I talk about filing divorce papers.

I go home and I call a lawyer to get information on what it takes to get a divorce. She tells me, "I'll be sending you two hundred and eighty-seven pages in which you will need to document all your financial information. I want you to write up another two hundred and eighty-seven pages of every cruel and abusive thing he's ever done to you."

"Um, he threw our fax machine," I offer.

"He threw the fax machine at you," she repeats.

"He threw it at the wall," I correct her.

"Did he throw it in your direction?" she pursues.

"Not really."

"How far from you did it land?"

"About eight feet," I say.

"Whew, that was close," she says, drawing in a deep breath, as if I'm lucky to be alive.

I WALK INTO the living room where my husband is reading the paper.

"I called a lawyer," I tell him.

He mutters, "Do what you have to do."

DOWNSTAIRS, A NEW couple comes in, and I begin with the standard questions: "Whose idea was it to come in? Who made the appointment?" I want to know who the resistant one is so I can acknowledge that.

The man says, "I don't think we need to be here."

I say, "Since you are the one who doesn't want to be here, what could we do, just for today, that would make the time useful for you?"

And what usually happens happens. He launches into his story and ends up talking much more than the one who *wanted* to come.

I'm able to work just fine, even though I worry that my sadness is a knowledge that passes through the air between my patients and me. I worry that I am contaminating them. I have a group that meets every week, and I have noticed that they've been in a prolonged state of grief.

"I am so sad," Violet says.

"So am I," says Laura.

"You think *you're* sad?" Ralph backhands.

Tamara weeps throughout the session.

I believe they are responding to me—to the life that they intellectually know nothing about, but because of blood knowledge, they feel. I blame myself for hurting them, for not standing up in group and saying, "It's me. I'm contagious. It's all my fault." I know I can't tell them. But I worry that I am poisoning my flock with my sad milk. I know I must do something about it.

I am mad at my own grandiosity, past and present. In

the past, when people asked me how to choose a therapist, I answered with certainty that you choose a therapist who is living a life you'd like to live. I thought that therapist was me. It makes me feel like a smart-ass, this voyage of self-discovery. I hate that I used to be so smug.

I don't want the life *I'm* living now.

What am I supposed to do about my patients when I feel like this, Lucy?

Send them home?

Lucy is no help. The better she makes me, the worse my marriage goes, the sorrier I feel for myself.

I only keep going to her for one reason: I love Lucy, and she loves me.

Lucy loves Sam, and Sam loves her.

Love makes the therapy chain strong. We hold on for dear life.

Colette and Timmy hold on, too. They hold me, and I won't let go. The problem is that, for now, Colette and Timmy are on the bottom of the therapy chain and no one is holding onto their feet. Their part of the therapy chain is incomplete. When someone grabs their feet, they will be secured in the completed circuit. Then, they'll get better, even if they feel worse.

·　·　·

why I stayed married: **reason #9**

HIS PET NAME for me became Shuggy Shughead. We got it from the noise a caboose makes. On St. Patrick's Day, he announced, "Today you are Shuggy O'Shughead." That year, he wrote me songs based on my new name. He would sing them for me and play them on his bass while I clapped. Sometimes I would go to hear him play at the Village Vanguard. One night, there on the stage with some of the best musicians around, there in the middle of a tune by Thelonious Monk, he slipped in two lines of "The Shuggy Shughead Song." We were the only ones who knew.

chapter 10

Couple's Therapy, Couple's Therapy, Couple's Therapy

While I was waiting to feel better, I was taking lots of medication. This relationship made me anxious, but so did staircases, subways, cellars, and everything else.

Soon I was becoming my own little CVS.

Trazadone gave me a raised paisley rash.

Navane didn't work.

Elavil made me fall asleep on the bandstand.

Restoril kept me in bed for days.

Ritalin made me clench my teeth.

Klonopin made it so I couldn't even masturbate.

Busbar made me laugh every time I said the name.

The list went on.

The marriage went on.

FINALLY, WE DECIDED to try couple's therapy. The first couple's therapist we saw was my husband's therapist, Lillian, who had no license to practice psychotherapy. Her husband was a psychiatrist, and he signed our bills so we could be reimbursed by our insurance companies. Her name wasn't even on them.

In New York, anyone can put out a shingle proclaiming, "I am a psychotherapist." But I think it is probably illegal to have someone who never met you sign your bill.

In our first session, she leaned back in her chair, crossed her thin legs, and struck the pose of therapeutic listening.

"And his apartment is a mess and there are holes in the wall . . . and . . . and . . . and . . ."

She replied, "Can you live with that?"

That was all she said, that psycho-puppet.

No matter what I said, that's what she said.

My small toehold of hope for the marriage, not to mention my sanity, was dissolving.

THE NEXT COUPLE'S therapist had an office full of tall African sculptures of naked men with pointy penises and naked women with pointy breasts. I decided from his art collection that he was a small-pricked sadist who cheated on his wife and got off by sexually arousing his patients. He had the tubby body and cavalier, bearded face of a roué, and he said his name was Eduardo, but I bet his mom called him Eddie.

"Before I start working with you," he said in a tone of superiority, "you'll have to answer one question: Are you a couple?"

I couldn't answer the question.

We sat in the most awkward silence.

I didn't like him or his genitalia menagerie. How could I trust him when he was obviously cheating on his wife with his statues?

THE NEXT COUPLE'S therapist saw us in his home while his wife, Sadie, cooked a chicken. The smells of Jewish cooking filled the air. He suggested that we talk and walk like apes. When my husband wanted to have sex, he should say, "Me want yum yum. Me want to kiss petunia." When I was angry, I should pound my chest and stick my butt in his face.

We dragged our knuckles across the floor of his office and giggled for a few weeks, until it wasn't funny anymore.

AFTER I STARTED graduate school, our couple's therapist experiences improved dramatically. Finally, we went to a couple's therapist who was our age, engaged to be married, and struggling to take the step of marriage himself. (He didn't say this, but we were his last appointment of the night. I saw her waiting for him. I saw the look in his eyes that always seemed to say, "Why is she always mad at me?")

This therapist said, "Well, you've been together and broken up for seven years. Breaking up hasn't seemed to end the relationship or to move it forward. Is it time to try something else, like putting both feet in the door and seeing what happens?"

I was relieved. This was different. I realized that I'd always had one foot out the door. I said so during every single fight: "I hate you. I'm leaving you." These words should have been printed on my pajamas.

I've always been amazed at couples who fight but who know deep inside that they love each other even when they are angry. I've never been that way. When I had a fight with my husband, I had a full-bodied do-or-die hate in me that I couldn't see beyond. I really believed I'd feel that way forever.

When I was younger, I turned the hate on myself, and that's why I got so self-destructive. Now, I could fully hate my husband and say horrible things to him instead of cutting myself with a razor blade.

This may have been progress, because one therapist told me, "Homicide is always better than suicide."

One issue that came up in the couple's therapy was that we had gotten stuck in an endless power struggle over our shoe-polish couch, and we'd never bought anything together since then—not a stick of furniture, not a pot roast pan, not a towel. This therapist gave us an assignment to buy a kitchen table together.

We'd gone seven years without a kitchen table, and he still had hope for us.

Go figure.

We started at Crate & Barrel, and we argued our way down to a secondhand furniture store on the Lower East Side. At Pottery Barn, we argued about the shape of the table. At Ikea, we argued about how many people it should seat. Our argument heated up at Bloomingdale's when we discussed what material the table should be made of, and we went over the top at Macy's when we tried to talk about whether or not to get chairs.

Exhausted, we bought a cheap, raw wood table that was never to be finished, never to have a chair, and more importantly, never to be used as a table.

When we reported this purchase to our therapist, he said, "How wonderful. Even though it was difficult, you ended up with a table."

This positive reinforcement felt great for both of us.

By the end of the first week, the table became just another place to stack boxes.

We never had a single meal at it.

. . .

why I stayed married: reason #10

MILTON NASCIMENTO, THE great Brazilian singer, was coming to the famous Blue Note jazz club. We loved Milton so much, but the show was a fortune—way above our budget. The cover charge alone was forty-five dollars per person. Still, we knew, just as a Jew must go to Israel, a Catholic must go to the Vatican, and a Muslim must go to Mecca, we must go to Milton.

The fervor of forbidden overspending is seductive and intense. We got to the Blue Note three hours early. It was open seating, and we wanted the best seats in the house.

We could count Milton's fillings, reach out and touch his guitar. At the end of the show, when he sang the Beatles' song, "Hello, Goodbye," my husband and I wept for every ounce of love and every ounce of loss we'd ever known.

I remembered how my husband had cried when Mimi died in *La Bohème*, how he'd sat on the edge of his seat, hoping beyond hope that this time she'd get well. I remembered how he'd cried when we listened to *Madame Butterfly*. Once, when my friend Livia was over, he played "Un Bel Di" for her. He explained the instrumentation. He translated the words. He conducted the CD player. The fervor built, and then he said, "Here, listen right here, that . . . and that . . ." He cried for pure beauty.

We decided to stay for Milton's second show, even though Milton sang the exact same songs in the exact same order. I can still taste the perfect safety, still feel the vein between my husband and me as Milton repeated that he didn't know why she was saying good-bye when he was saying hello.

chapter 11

My Patient Comes a Few Times During Intercourse

*D*uring my marriage, two things changed: First, instead of saying, "I hate you," now I could say, "I hate you. I want a divorce." Next, I began to study my couples differently. I wanted to believe that my husband and I were no worse off than anyone else. I turned the other couples into barometers. In the past, my comparative study was always between my current partner and my former partners. That gave me a lot to work with, but this new study was an improvement. As a therapist, I could view relationships that didn't include me. I could observe how others fought and repaired.

I kept a weekly log of dissatisfactions and distresses. I listened for what made us similar and what made us different. I was desperate to find out where we were situated on the relationship bell curve.

CASE 32

Names:	Anita and Henry
Ages:	Late 30s
Relationship:	Married six years
Children:	No children
Reason for treatment:	Think they shouldn't be together

"We've been married for six years, and I think about divorce every day. We have nothing in common. He was never my type. I don't even want to have sex with him," Anita tells me. "He's clumsy, and he's big, and he gets too excited. It's like trying to make love to a St. Bernard puppy. He slobbers."

Henry smiles. "I am big. I can't help that. But I'm willing to do or try anything she wants anyway she wants. She's the boss of this," he says, devilishly gesturing toward his groin.

Anita giggles. "See? He's crude. I forgot to mention he's crude. Did I ever mention you're crude?" she says, turning to him and pointing her finger in his face.

"The thing is that she's so unwilling to let me have her that, when I do, I get overexcited," Henry says, grabbing her finger like it's a penis and jerking it off. "It's like a million men trying to get out of the same revolving door at the same time."

She sticks out her tongue at him. He tries to grab it.

Anita adds, "It's not like I'm totally unsatisfied. I always come a few times during intercourse."

Henry butts in, "Yeah, there's no problem for her there. But what about me? She comes so fast. Boom, boom, boom. I'm just getting started, and she's lying there waiting for me to come. I start to feel pressured."

"Like a lump," she adds. "You forgot to say I lie like a lump."

"She has no interest in my orgasm. She waits for it to be over. She makes it hard for me to come. It's hard to come when your wife couldn't care less."

A few times? During intercourse? She's complaining about sex, and she comes a few times during intercourse? In that regard, they are way ahead of my husband and me. But we wouldn't be so mean to each other in front of someone else. We only do that in private.

Anita and Henry:	-1 for being mean to each other in front of me
Me and my husband:	+1 for only being mean to each other in private
Anita and Henry:	+1 for having sex
Me and my husband:	-1 for not having sex

Anita is saying, "We met at a friend's party. And we had a few dates. It was never hot and heavy. But after a few dates my period was late. Henry brought home one of those drugstore pregnancy tests. It showed positive. So we got married a few days later. Then, I got my period. I don't know whether I lost the baby or I got a screwed-up test kit. But you see? You see what I mean? We never *decided* to be together. We got duped into being together."

Henry is nodding in agreement. "I never would have married her otherwise," he says with vigor. "The girl I was seeing before her . . . now *she* was my type."

Do they expect me to believe they were duped into marriage? Perhaps they thought they had a compelling reason to get married, but that isn't the same as being duped. Who duped them into forgetting to have safer sex? My husband and I were anything but duped.

> Anita and Henry: -1 for impulsive marriage
> Me and my husband: -1 for impulsive marriage

"And another thing," Anita says. "I want him to stop reading his porn mags in bed when I'm trying to sleep."

"I'd do it in the living room, but Anita doesn't want to get into bed alone. She gets lonely. She wants me there. She insists that we get into bed at the same time."

After suggesting that Henry negotiate for a little time alone with his magazines in the living room, I say to Henry, "Are you comfortable with that?"

"Oh, I like it," Henry says. "I want to go to bed at the same time. But she's gonna have to get used to me masturbating."

There's another difference. I do want to get into bed alone. I do want to stay in bed alone. I do want to wake up alone.

Anita and Henry:	+1 for wanting to sleep together
Me and my husband:	-1 for wanting to sleep apart

Anita and Henry:	+1 for her not being furious that he reads porn
Me and my husband:	-1 for my getting furious about porn even though we aren't having sex

Henry is still speaking. "I think she should get earplugs."

Anita snaps, "You know I can't wear earplugs. I have tinnitus." She turns to me and says, "See what I mean? Why does he have to do this? We shouldn't be together."

"She's right," Henry says. "I should have married the woman I was seeing before Anita." He launches into a description of the woman who would have been better for him—who would have made him happier.

Anita and Henry:	+1 for believing that happiness is possible
Me and my husband:	-1 for having no such belief

Six months later, Anita is pregnant again. "I can go and live with my mother if me and Henry don't work out.

Henry isn't sure he wants the baby. He doesn't think that after being duped into getting married that we should be duped into staying together."

"She's right. I'm not cut out for this. I never was. And I will not be able to watch her get fat."

"We're going to turn the office into a nursery. Henry's mom's friend has a load of baby clothes for us," Anita says to me. Then she turns to Henry and says, "Watch *me* get fat? Look down, baby. You haven't seen your own dick in five years."

Henry taps his belly. Then he taps Anita's belly. Then he leans over and puts his ear to it. "I hear something," he announces, though we all know this isn't true.

"Yeah, well, listen good," Anita tells him. She puts her hand on his head.

Anita and Henry:	+1 for being unable to keep their hands off each other
Me and my husband:	-1 for no touching

I listen to Anita and Henry good. I listen good to the perplexing way they conduct a marriage.

In another month, I listen to their pain. Anita and Henry are collapsed on my couch.

"Lost the baby," she says.

Henry bursts into tears that spray like Old Faithful. He lays his head in her lap. She cradles him, tucking her fingers beneath his chin. He reaches up gently to touch her hair. Their tenderness is a force. Their tenderness is a spell. I drift toward them like a lonely, thirsty stranger riding into a new town.

Anita strokes Henry gently. She grabs a tissue and tells him to blow. He blows his nose; she wipes it and puts the tissue in her purse.

Anita says, "How could we raise a kid, anyway, when we don't even know if we're going to stay together?"

FINAL SCORE AND ASSESSMENT
Anita and Henry: +3
Me and my husband: -5

Anita and Henry share everything, even their suffering.
My husband and I suffer alone.

Anita and Henry have tried to be unhappy with each other, but they can't.
My husband and I have tried to be happy with each other, but we can't.

•   •   •

why I stayed married: **reason #11**

WE'D HAD THE biggest snowstorm New York City had seen in years, and our unequipped city shut down. My husband and I had a whole day off together, something we always cherished. We decided to dress really warmly and walk to Battery Park, where you can see the Statue of Liberty and Ellis Island. We thought the snow would be deepest in the park, where no one had plowed. We wanted to make snow angels there.

Crossing the park, we could barely see the benches buried under huge drifts. The snow was up to our thighs as we approached Castle Clinton, the place where George Washington holed up during the Revolutionary War. As we trudged by a decrepit part of the castle with big holes in the walls, my husband noticed a cardboard box stuffed in one of the holes. He walked over to the box, where the snow was nearly up to his waist.

"Is someone in there?" he asked.

A male voice answered, "Yes."

"Are you OK?" my husband asked.

"No," the voice responded. "My wife and I have been stuck in here for way over a day. We have no food. She's very cold. We're snowed in and can't dig out."

My husband yelled, "Don't worry. We'll get you food and help. We're going to leave, but we'll come right back."

Together, we ran to find a phone, and we called 911. Then we ran to a deli. He bought hot soup and crackers and candy and whatever else we could carry. We ran back to the castle, and, as we approached, the police were already there, taking the couple into a waiting ambulance. My husband walked over to the man he'd spoken with and handed him the bag filled with food.

The two men's eyes met, like at the end of a movie about Iwo Jima: a disaster, a rescue, survivors—a bond that the rest of us never fully understand.

I threw my arms around my husband as we walked back into the park. He was the greatest. I thought of all the people who would have walked by the big cardboard box and never thought to say a word.

We fell onto our backs in the snow and made a thousand snow angels, our arms and legs flapping angel after angel after angel into existence.

chapter 12

We Get a Dog to Try to Save the Marriage

And so the years passed . . . eight . . . nine . . . ten . . . eleven. We settled in, setting up tactical boundaries, although a word was never spoken, no formal lines drawn.

I slept in the bedroom.

He slept in the living room until we moved, and then he slept in the basement.

I had one phone line.

He had another.

I ate alone.

He never ate in front of me—not even a slice of bread.

I woke up early and wrote.

He slept until ten minutes before he had to leave the house. Then came the thrashing, running, dripping, everywhere at once. A blitz of wet towel balls, unmatched cuff links, lost suspenders, shuffled sheet music, the blowing of snot. And he was gone.

He did not come home until two or three or four in the morning. I would hear the clamor of a door being knocked open by a bass wheel. It could be two or three or four days before I actually saw him as more than a blur whizzing in or out the door.

Every month, I'd have lunch with my friends Charles and Ross. We'd talk about what movies we'd seen. We'd make each other laugh. We'd talk about who was writing what, working on what. We'd exchange book ideas. We'd talk and talk and talk, and I would never once say, without stupidly joking, that I was miserable.

Why did I choose to live like this?

This is not an easy question to answer when a relationship with no sex and no kitchen table is by far the best relationship you've ever had.

Part of the answer is that, for me, having a guy I never saw was a step up. Although I never thought about it much, I seemed to need a man. Before meeting my husband, I frequently went from one guy to another with little regard for character.

Take, for instance, an old alcoholic boyfriend. He plowed his fancy sports car into the railing on the passenger side, the side where I was sitting. I am not forgetting that I got in the car with him when he was dead drunk. After I broke my collarbone and dislocated my shoulder, did I dump this lush?

He came to see me in the hospital on the day when fluid filled my lungs. I sounded like a broken humidifier. He tried to stick his hand inside my hospital johnny. My gurgling did not bother him at all. He came again to see me at my mother's house a couple of days after I got out of the hospital. He licked my ear. My collarbone was taped up.

"I'm sick," I told him.

"I've got to have you," was his reply.

Men had desired me before, but this was the first time anyone ever said he had to have me. I was surprised when he was not careful with my dressings, when he moved me ways that hurt.

"This is hurting me."

"I've got to have you," he repeated, tightening his grip on my shoulder when I tried to pull away.

When he left, I discovered that all my pain pills were missing.

I guess he had to have them, too.

I should stop right here and go back to my husband, many steps up.

As I said, we'd successfully put ourselves on different schedules so there was as little contact as possible. When we did bump into each other, I'd tell him, "I'm unhappy." He'd say, "Your unhappiness is my only problem."

Do you know what it is like to be enraged twenty-four hours a day?

To have trouble falling asleep, even with your sleeping pills, because you're so goddamn mad?

To wake up and have your very first thought be that you're furious?

To hide your towel in the bedroom so he can't use it?

And, while this is how you feel *all* the time, do you know what it's like to be with a husband who swears he is happy and says that all he wants is for you to be happy?

How can my *husband* be happy if *I'm* not?

How can I divorce a happily married man?

My neurosis kicked like a frightened goat backed into a corner. I began to think about having a baby. Does this surprise you? Remember, I was the one who bought my husband a new car to stop him from fucking up the couch. But at my age, having a trying-to-save-the-marriage-baby was out of the question, although I did bring up the subject of adoption. He had absolutely no interest, and there was a part of me that was sure no one would give us a baby if they had any sense at all.

Having a family was never the point of our being together.

Neither was being happy.

Still, I needed something.

And that was when I began to think about my patient, Jane.

JANE IS IN love with her dog, Shadow.

"This is Shadow when he was a baby," she says, her hair like a big, black, cumulus cloud, as she shows me the picture that she carries in her wallet. "And this is Shadow on Halloween," as she shows me a Scottie in a skeleton outfit.

"His belly smells like baking bread," she tells me and bursts into tears. "That's the only time I'm really happy . . . the *only* time."

She loves Shadow's vocal eases that tell her he likes his breakfast and his squeaky banana toy. She loves when Shadow sleeps on his back with his four stumpy legs up in the air, like a table base in search of a slab of glass. She loves walking Shadow up and down her block as people ooh and aah at his goofy terrier puss, as doormen offer cookies to Shadow and lusty smiles to Jane.

Jane doesn't take vacations unless Shadow can come. She won't celebrate Thanksgiving or Christmas or New Year's Eve without him. Jane is in love with her dog, and although she's not having sex with him, she's not having sex with anyone else either. "I'd marry him . . . if he'd have me."

I have never felt this kind of love, let alone seen it up close. I can't imagine.

Loving Shadow is not Jane's problem. Everyone knows what's going on between them. She has scared away more than one man with graphic details of expelling Shadow's anal glands. Jane's problem is that she has been in mourning for Shadow since the day the breeder handed him to her. In her mind, every day is the day Shadow will die. She can easily tell me that she and Shadow may register at Bloomingdale's, but it's embarrassing to burst into tears over Shadow's death when he is only three years old and as healthy as a horse. He's never been sick a day in his life, but Jane has paid for two CAT scans. After all, Shadow can't tell her what hurts.

At this point, I wonder why Jane would pick me for a therapist. I don't have a dog, nor would I ever want one. I hate dog breath. Dogs smell. In New York City, where I live, you have to pick up their poop.

Every day, I see dogs of every shape and size squat over puddles and piles. I have to avert my eyes or get nauseated. I also hate seeing those pet owners in their designer suits and dresses using *The New York Times* or little plastic sandwich bags to pick up dog poop. It makes me gag to watch how they maneuver the poop to a trash can.

Once, I made the mistake of mentioning the poop to Jane. She smiled as if I were a fourth grader who just learned where the penis goes. She said, "It's a labor of love."

A labor of love? *A labor of love?* What about the homeless who recycle soda cans out of the trash so they can buy food? Is it fair for them to come up with a Pepsi can covered with dog poop? What about the trash collectors who have it hard enough without having to scrape poop off their gloves? What about me-me-me-me-me who has to watch this grossness every day?

Jane wakes up early every day to take Shadow to the dog run before she goes to work. There, amidst the slobbery bulldogs and skinny hounds, there, where every dog takes its morning dump, there, where the dogs roll in the dirtiest dirt and then rub up against you, Jane actually eats a muffin, drinks coffee, and calls it the best part of her day.

During that quality time, is Jane happy?

In the middle of her most exquisite joy, Jane imagines herself in the vet's office singing softly to Shadow, holding his limp paw, his life passing before her eyes.

Well, isn't that the truth of all great love?

One dies first.

These are the real facts of life.

The best that love has to offer is also the worst pain we'll ever know.

ONE NIGHT, WHILE my husband is thrashing around trying to get out of the house, I announce, "I want a dog."

"No dog," he says and wheels his bass out the door.

But would I, who could go out and buy a house without consulting my husband, be daunted by his not wanting a dog?

I go to the pet store and come home with books about breeds.

As I flip through the books, I begin to feel like a desperate mother trying to find her child.

Jane, Jane, Jane. All I can think about is my dog, dog, dog.

I corner my husband and tell him that we must have a dog.

I corner my husband and tell him that he can name the dog.

I corner my husband and tell him that I cannot live without a dog.

After weeks of working on him as Michelangelo must have worked on his David, hacking away everything that is not David, not dog, something falls from his lips, tiny as a poppy seed off a bagel.

"Sparky," he murmurs.

As if Sparky were the code word, I immediately call the American Kennel Club and get names of breeders. I find puppies two hours away and insist we drive that night to see them. I arrive with cash in my pocket.

When I see Sparky, a space opens in my heart, a space I did not know was there. For the first time in my life, I surrender to love. I love everything in him and even everything that comes out of him. One touch, my head on his belly—it is all like a drug. My past no longer matters much to me. I have a puppy. And he was worth it all.

WHEN JANE COMES to therapy the following week, I tell her about my Cairn terrier puppy, Sparky Jones, who lies on his back and enters an ecstatic trance when I rub his belly. I thank Jane for her miraculous gift to me.

We exchange photos.

Within months, Sparky gets a little sister named Scarlett.
We count the years.
Her dog is four. My dogs are one.
Her dog is five. My dogs are two.
Her dog is six. My dogs are three.
When Jane weeps, I weep with her.

. . .

why I stayed married: **reason #12**

MY FRIEND HAD lost her hair to chemotherapy. We sat in her living room, and next to her sat a brown wig on a wig stand while she wore a kerchief over her hairless head. She was muddling through rejoining the world, but she had concerns.

"I want to go out but I don't want to go out in the kerchief—it screams *cancer* and I don't want the stares. But I think I look stupid in the wig. Just stupid."

"No," my husband said. "*You* don't look stupid in the wig." And he took it off the stand and carefully placed it on his own head. "*I* look stupid in the wig."

We laughed and laughed. My friend put on the wig, and we all went out for lunch.

chapter 13

A Drawer That Won't Close

*A*s a child, I had a wooden toy that had eight drawers in eight different colors. When you pushed one drawer in, another popped out. Over and over again, I tried to push all the drawers in, holding them with multiple fingers, pushing them against the floor, but there was only one right combination, one right order that would permit me to close all the drawers at the same time.

Many of my patients visit me that way, with a drawer that won't close for them—the lost-love drawer, the angry-wife drawer, the I-hate-my-boss-but-I-make-too-much-money-to-quit-my-job drawer, the I-always-give-more-than-I-get drawer. I have learned that we must unpack these drawers before they will close. This involves looking behind them, because, usually, something is stuck back there. An old sock, a dirty magazine, a forbidden wish, an unmet need.

Sure, you can leave the drawer open, or try to shove it or nail it or ignore it. Some of us can actually forget it—and put all our stuff in the other drawers. Usually, when someone comes to see me, they've already tried that, and it didn't work.

ADAM COMES TO see me with the I've-got-everything-but-love drawer open. He doesn't know why it won't close for him. He loves women—their smell, their bodies, their scars. He tells me that when they want to come but are worried that it's taking too long, he'll say, "I'm right here with you," until they dissolve in arousal and gratitude. So why is he a forty-year-old fuck buddy who's never had a girl-friend for longer than two months?

Adam considers many possibilities to answer this question, and he can't be loyal to any of them. How hasn't he met the right one yet when everyone else he knows has? Could there be no right one? Is he doomed to live alone? What if he's fallen in love, but he doesn't know it? Or, the scariest possibility of all: What if he *can't* fall in love? What if he can't feel love at all?

Meanwhile, I ask myself: Why did I fall in love with my husband? Why have I been with him for fifteen years? Why couldn't we have just suffered together for five years and then moved on? OK, he was a bass player and I was a singer. OK, I loved jazz and he played jazz extremely well. OK, he was kind of famous and I sang flat. OK, he had a great, brainy wit and that brooding, mysterious quality I used to go for.

Adam is reluctant to unpack the drawer, while I can think of nothing else. He wants me to soothe him and tell him that he just hasn't met the right woman. How can I soothe him when I can't soothe myself?

When my office hours are over and I walk upstairs, I have to face facts: My bad-marriage-but-scared-to-leave drawer is popping out.

Worse: I've called a lawyer, but I'm scared to make an appointment.

And even worse: My husband doesn't believe I really did it, even though I told him I really did it. He still thinks we can save the marriage. He thinks that mediation, if we go, will be a place for him to talk about what went wrong, a place where I'll reconsider. He still thinks a mediator is just one more on our long list of marriage counselors. He still thinks I'm going through a phase. He's blamed our condo, my therapist, Lucy, my friend Carol. He is sure my wish to break up is like all our other breakups—temporary. He will not hear otherwise. We fight. He stands in front of the television waving his arms and yelling while I'm trying to watch my favorite program. He looms over me while I try to eat breakfast. He stomps on the floor when I am right below him with a patient.

I ask Adam to tell me about his longest relationship. He tells me that his longest relationship lasted two months. She was a kind and beautiful ballerina. She adored him. But she made the terrible mistake of leaving him alone in her bedroom while she went to make breakfast. Snooping, he read her diary. On June 21, six months before they met, she'd thought about doing it with two men at the same time. She never did it, she wrote, she just thought it.

Adam grabbed the diary and stormed into the kitchen. He ended it right then and there as the shocked dancer, who was eating breakfast, dissolved into tears with cereal in her teeth.

Even Adam can see that it was a ridiculous reason to dump her.

But he doesn't miss her. He just never hangs around long enough to get attached.

One thing about my husband is that he is totally attached—nothing is going to make him leave me. I've begun to see his refusal to leave me as hostility, not love. Then I remember what I thought when I was in the hospital—that if I discovered tomorrow that I had to have both of my breasts removed, he wouldn't blink. Then again, I can't remember the last time he actually saw both my breasts. Then again, I can't remember the last time I really cared about that, or even about whether I had breasts.

I decide to try telling him again, with more conviction: "I'm—getting—a—divorce. We have to go to mediation."

As coldly as a biology student pithing a frog, he tells me

he's changed his mind. Now he refuses to go because going to mediation suggests that he agrees the marriage is over. He doesn't agree that it is.

"Agree? Agree? What is there to agree to?" I start screaming. "My ring's been off my finger for a year. We haven't slept in the same room for a year. We haven't had dinner together in a year, or sex in more than five. You can't have a marriage all by yourself!"

"I'm late for work, and I can't find my bow tie," he responds, rising quickly and leaving the room.

"This is not a marriage!" I yell as he wheels the bass out the door, then runs back in because he forgot his music. He gathers his music as I scream at the top of my lungs.

When he comes home at two in the morning, he wakes me up so he can have his side of the screaming match.

"I will fight you. The house will be sold. You don't actually think I'd let you stay here. I will never let you stay here. I will take Sparky. You won't get him."

"I'm not supposed to be married," I weep. "I'm not supposed to be married."

I ask Adam, "Are you supposed to get married?"

"Are you kidding?" Adam says. "My parents are dying for grandchildren. They're elderly, in their eighties, and they tell me they don't have long. I'd better hurry up. And I want to. I can't think of anything more awful than them not getting their grandchildren. It's all up to me."

"Your parents started their family late," I comment.

Adam casually explains that both of his parents are

Holocaust survivors. He tells me he grew up in a community of Holocaust survivors: the butcher, the baker, and the dentist, the other students in his class—all Holocaust survivors or children of Holocaust survivors. He spent summers in the Catskills with Holocaust survivors. In fact, it wasn't until he was nine or ten that he knew there were any people besides Holocaust survivors.

I suggest to him that we look at his family history and how it might impact his life today. I tell him that it's the only way I can wrap my mind around his problem.

"That's ridiculous," he says. "What do my parents have to do with the fact that I can't find a girlfriend? There's no connection."

"Maybe not," I say, "but we have to start somewhere. It'll help me, even if it won't help you."

"Look," Adam tries to explain, "my family's situation was so much better than most people's I grew up with. My mother lost her whole family, but my father hid in the forest with his brothers and my grandfather. They fought in the Polish resistance, which, mind you, is a story he loves to tell over and over. They hardly lost anyone."

"Who did they lose?" I ask.

"Just his mother and his sister. Just the females. All the men survived. Now tell me what you think this has to do with dating, because I think it's a waste of time." He tugs his tie in frustration.

What will it take to convince Adam that his status as the child of Holocaust survivors may have something to do with his romantic struggles? What will it take to convince my husband that I'm out and there is no turning back this time? What will it take for me to cope with my profound feelings of loss?

In the following weeks, indulging me and annoyed with me, Adam talks about his classroom full of survivors, the parties full of survivors, the temple full of survivors—then he tries to tell me that he's not depressed. It's his Eastern European state of mind, like the joke: How many people does it take to change a Jewish grandmother's light bulb? None, she'll sit in the dark.

"I'm a fatalist," he says, "a pragmatist. How could I get depressed after what my parents went through? What do you think they're gonna say if I say, 'Y'know, I feel bad. I'm not happy because I have a pimple,' or, 'Geez, my hair is thinning on top—it's so upsetting.' I've never had an unhappy day. I'm the happiest guy I know."

As he speaks, I drift into the climate in the house when he was born. A woman in her forties is pregnant. Was this her first child or could there have been another whole family that Adam doesn't even know about? I have heard many stories about men and women who, after having lost everyone in the war, began new families and never spoke of it to their new children.

A mother-to-be wants her mother at a time like this. She needs a mother to call, a mother to complain to about her ankles, a mother to come and stay with her, a mother to guide her through this phase of her life. A mother-to-be wants the baby shower that her sisters should be throwing her, her nieces' and nephews' hand-me-downs, a cousins club.

There are none.

Adam's birth, this most joyous birth, is also the most painful reminder.

No grandparents ever, no one to send baby pictures to.

No mother to tell you how hard it was when she was pregnant with you—to remind you of your birth, to compare her grandchild's first words with your first words.

My mind slips from the past to the future, to Adam walking down the aisle with his mother and father on each arm—walking to meet his beautiful bride. Tears are rolling down his mother's face as he kisses her, as his parents hand him over to another woman. His mother's mascara is smearing. She has lost her position as the number one woman in his life. She is watching her only son walk away.

More loss.

I tell Adam I think his parents have lost enough. He can't get married. His mother cannot bear to lose any more.

"That has to be the most ridiculous thing I've ever heard," Adam says, and this time, he's really annoyed. "My parents aren't even here most of the year. They go to Florida."

"What is most ridiculous about it?" I ask.

"I don't even see them that much. I mean, I take my mother to her doctor because my father can't drive anymore. Besides, he won't listen to her, but that's nothing new. She needs someone to talk to, so we talk. All he does these days is tell the same stories over and over again. All she does is shop and ask me when I'm going to give her grandchildren. They can be pretty annoying actually, but, if I know one thing, it's how much they want me to be happy."

"Have you brought any of your dates home to meet them?" I ask.

"I used to. So far, they really have liked everyone I've introduced them to—but they just didn't think any of them were right to marry. I brought home Sarah, the paralegal I told you about. My mother liked her. Sarah spent six hours listening to my father talk about the Polish resistance. He loved her. They didn't think she was educated enough. The only reason they didn't like Faye was that she didn't keep kosher."

I repeat what I said: "You must never make your mother give you away."

Adam walks out the door thinking I must be daft.

I climb the stairs. My husband is hunched over the computer. He quickly hits the button that hides the porn site, the place he goes when he says he is doing his online banking.

I say, "If you don't go to mediation with me, I'm going to a divorce lawyer. I mean it this time." My husband looks at me like I must be daft. Indeed, I've only said this 632 times before.

Every day for six weeks, I look at the lawyer's phone number and choke.

On the seventh week, I am sitting in a lawyer's office filling out papers, and Adam has met someone. He knew the moment he saw her that he'd been waiting for her all his life. As he speaks of this bolt of lightning called love, I learn the elegant fashion in which his unconscious has solved the problem of finding a woman to love and remaining true to his mom. I learn what makes this girl different from all other girls.

"She moved here from Israel, and she eats like a bird," he tells me. "Tiny, the tiniest, skinniest thing you ever saw—maybe eighty pounds—that's all she weighs. Not one ounce more. In fact, it's a worry. Who could survive on the little she eats?"

A few months later, Adam will marry a survivor, while I wonder if I will survive the wait for my husband to be served with divorce papers.

Case closed.

Drawer shut.

.   .   .

why I stayed married: **reason #13**

THE TWO OF us would drive to a swamp to see the turtles or go to a park to see the geese. Our friends thought we were weird, driving three hours to see a duck with a red tuft on its head, trudging through muck to find a toad, or tripping on tree stumps to follow a pileated woodpecker through the Maine woods. We were happiest when we were in the woods.

By far the most difficult hike we took was four and a half miles down and then four and a half miles up the side of the Grand Canyon at the end of May. We hadn't planned it at all. We started talking to a German couple and they were walking down, so we joined them. Down was fun, and we never gave a thought to up. We had enough water, but we only brought carrot sticks to eat.

It only took us two hours to walk down, but it took three times as long going up. It was hot as only the Grand Canyon can be. We passed a man who was throwing up and a woman who'd been sitting in the same spot for three hours. People who weren't even breathless passed us. We could only go a few feet at a time. I refused to pee because there was no privacy. It didn't matter that much because, even though we drank and drank, we were dehydrated. We conserved the carrot sticks even though we were starving.

Then, for the last two miles, he said he really didn't want any carrot sticks. He'd had a much bigger breakfast than I had had, and he was feeling fine. He kept plying me with water and making me drink. He said he'd had so much water already, he didn't need as much of that either. Thirty feet from the top, he started making goofy talk. His face was red, and he looked dazed. He said he was going to sit for a minute, but I should keep going. We looked up and the German couple was waiting for us with cold sodas in their hands. They'd been there for hours. I went up, and when I looked back, he was still sitting there. It took him another hour to climb those last thirty feet.

He was hallucinating—totally dehydrated. He was sick— red-faced and vomiting. He told me he'd given the water and carrots to me because he was so worried about me.

That night, as I soaked in the tub, I knew that I would have stayed with him on the Titanic. He was the only life-boat I needed.

When he pulled me out of the tub, I was still so sore.

"I brought the peppermint cream you love," he said. "Want a foot rub?"

chapter 14

My Psyche Reads Like a Sandwich Board

I haven't told my patients that I'm getting a divorce. Only Charlene has commented on the fact that I stopped wearing my wedding ring almost a year ago. Charlene watches. She knows if my mind wanders off during a session. She catches every mistake I make. She drinks me in. She comments on my new shoes, a book taken off a bookshelf, a new shade of foundation that uplifts the eye area, the odd shape of the spot on my forearm. To Charlene, my psyche reads like a sandwich board.

Several times in the past months she's fingered her purple curls and made comments such as, "I'm worried.

You're unhappy, and you don't like men. That's why you aren't encouraging me to date. My social life is suffering because you can't get along with your husband."

Last week she said, "Look, Sharyn, I know you've been married three times, but I haven't been married even once. I want to get married, and your bitterness is stopping me. I need a new shrinker."

One night on a Jewish holiday, when the regular host wanted off, I got asked to guest host on WABC radio's call-in talk show from 11 p.m. to 5 a.m. At 2 a.m., on line one, a voice said, "Hi, Sharyn. Charlene here. You know, I asked you a question in our last session, and I didn't like your answer, so I want to ask you again now."

Every week, Charlene arrives early, knocks on my consultation room door, and asks me to see her right away. Every week, I escort her back to the waiting room until her noon appointment time. I open my door at noon and, within two minutes, I become the flight attendant who gets sucked out of the airplane's emergency exit in one of those bad airplane movies.

Do you know that feeling, that feeling of being with someone who can't get enough air or light or food? In seconds, starving Charlene has eaten all of my furniture, all of my walls. Yet I fail to fill or satisfy Charlene. I am the Red Cross truck that never arrived, so she eats dirt. I am a big, white stove with pots of delicious food simmering on top. Charlene reaches for me, and she gets burnt.

She muses, "I haven't seen your husband. I always used

to see him carrying his bass fiddle out. C'mon, Sharyn. This is me. It's Charlene here. Do you have something to tell me? Don't you owe me an honest relationship?"

It's been a year. Is Charlene really the only one who notices that my wedding ring is gone? Is everyone else just too polite to say? Or, are they afraid that my getting a divorce will mean that I can't pay attention to them and only Charlene has the nerve to spell that out in black and white? What about my neighbors? Even though my husband disappeared three months ago, only one couple has commented on that. I feel as if I've sprouted another nose, and everyone is doing his or her best not to stare.

I should just spit it out—turn to them and say, "Good morning. I dumped the turd." I'm certainly not the first therapist to get a divorce.

Ouch! I'm not *a* therapist. I'm *the* therapist who wrote *How to Stay Lovers for Life: Discover a Marriage Counselor's Tricks of the Trade*. I'm the therapist who went on CNN to debate with Arianna Huffington about the state of marriage in America. There was Arianna talking about communication as the most vital part of a marriage, while I was talking about who cleans the toilet in a marriage. Arianna and I had two different kinds of failed marriages. I had to wonder about the producer who chose us out of all the women in America to be the ones to discuss marriage.

I'm the therapist who peppered her book with darling anecdotes about her own quaint marriage—sweet little fables of what I did when my husband refused to make the bed or forgot to buy me an anniversary card. I'm the therapist who never appeared on television without the host asking me about my husband—because I talk about him in my books. I was filled with such affection for him. I always had a funny story to tell. I took him or the idea of him everywhere. I'm the therapist to whom my dear friend Alexia, as she was dying, said, "Your book is a love letter to your husband."

A love letter? A love letter? I didn't have the heart to tell Alexia, but I think that a love letter to your husband presupposes that it will be read by him.

When I asked him for the ten thousandth time to read a chapter from my book on marriage counseling and tell me what he thought, he, as usual, fell asleep on the couch with the big black stains.

I, as usual, acted surprised to find him three hours later still holding the first page. He, as usual, said, "I don't know about these things."

I, as usual, said, "But you know me," and, as usual, I started the usual fight as my usual heart felt suckerpunched and he, as usual, felt attacked by the red-haired monkey changeling who, as usual, thrashed and sputtered and claimed to be his wife.

This is where we live now: on a stained couch where past and present have lost meaning. Our dream of a safe space together, a place where all lost shoes are quickly found, a place where there are no staircases anywhere—all of this is gone. And in its place are our childhood nightmares.

For eternity, my husband sits on a step watching the others kids drive away.

For eternity, I am one of the kids in the car, giggling happily, making a face out the window.

For eternity, I stand at the bottom of an endless flight of stairs with that motherfucker at my back.

For eternity, my husband is the one who never comes to get me out of the basement.

He almost catches me hiding his shoe in a drawer.

I almost catch him leaning against the cellar door so I can't get out.

The tragedy is that, with all the hope we brought to each other, it has come to this.

Charlene, Charlene, I was so hungry for my husband, so starving for his approval, so desperate for him to be interested in me, so rabid for him to let me out of the cellar and scare the little buzzards away. Charlene, I know what it's like not to take no for an answer. I wouldn't stop trying to get him to read my work, because he always had such smart ideas. But he gave them to me like they were the last sips of water in the world, and I was his bratty, demonic sister. I was going crazy. *Is that what I do to you?*

It was like that even when we first got involved, and I was singing. Why did it take me so long to notice? When I met him, I thought I was a good singer—never a great one, but solid. The guys in the band liked me and my singing. We hooked up. I knew lots of songs—interesting songs they liked to play. I was easy to get along with on a gig. I was more than happy to go to the bar during a long set and return to the bandstand with whatever anyone wanted. I could balance four gin and tonics and a plate of hot hors d'oeuvres at one time.

SOON AFTER WE met, I got a weeklong gig in a little club outside Boston, and I hired my husband to play bass for me. I was so excited that we were working together. I invited my family and my friends. This famous New York bass player was going to be spending a week with me on a bandstand.

During the first set of the first night, I turned to smile at him a few times, but he wasn't looking at me.

He was miserable.

At first he said, "The piano player's chords—they're making me nervous."

But by our third night together, he'd stopped speaking to me. I knew it had nothing to do with the piano player. He couldn't listen to me singing—my voice, my intonation, my tempos. I bothered him. When I was singing the bridge of "Bewitched, Bothered and Bewildered," I looked into his eyes and saw the eyes of a man who had left the room twenty minutes ago.

Later that night, he tried to teach me the correct bridge to "Don't Blame Me." "You're changing the notes on the bridge, and you can't do that until you know the bridge. Do you know how many guys can't play the melody to a song? They play over the changes, but they never learn the tune. That's cheating."

"My notes fit," I protested meekly.

"That's not the point." And he sang the bridge over and over and over until I started crying. He became more intense, meaner—like a scary drill sergeant.

He sang a note. "Can you hear that?"

I could not.

It hit me—that look in his eye was the same look my father had when I broke my arm, the same look my mother had when I wanted to get out of my grandmother's bedroom. I was an imposition. I was that scab you know you shouldn't pick but you want to anyway.

After that, as soon as I could, I stopped singing for good.

I never even sang a song when I was alone at home, or in the car on a long ride.

I could not bear to hear what he heard when he heard me.

CHARLENE, KEEP LETTING me have it until I give you what you want.

Don't let me off the hook.

Be better at this than I am.

I am learning a thing or two from you.

Because, you know, I tried working him like you work me.

I was not going to give up on getting him to notice me.

I paced my asking.

I tried asking different times of the day. Maybe mornings were bad.

I tried asking different days of the week.

I tried Post-it notes.

I tried asking every day.

I tried asking ten times a day.

I tried screaming at the top of my lungs.

I tried name-calling.

I tried calling his mother to tell her what a terrible husband he was.

I tried antidepressants.

I tried not trying.

Now, I'm trying divorce.

CHARLENE, THANK YOU, but I am still outraged that you, whom I have seen for forty-five minutes once a week for three years, know more and care more about my feelings than does my husband, with whom I have lived for fifteen years. At least you know I have my feelings, whether you guess right or wrong as to what they are. It's unfortunate that you always guess right.

I can't please Charlene, and she pays me on time. My husband can't please me, and he pays half the mortgage. Neither one wants to leave me, even though I am not making them happy. On either side of my therapy door, nothing I do is right.

Today Charlene tells me that I feed her bad food. She'd like to punch my tit, hoping that punching my tit might work like banging the television. "You don't have milk in your breasts," she informs me, "you have shit." She tastes shit, but she'll take it and try to turn it into milk. Feed me, she screams, her mouth a big Muncho.

Love me, I scream at my husband when I'm on the other side of my door. I take shit and try to turn it into love.

Charlene and I float where lost souls float, never touching each other, in the place where no one asks how your day was.

My husband never thought about how my day was before he saw me because, for him, there *was* no before he saw me. He carried me in his head all the time, like a bulbous attachment, a goiter, an overarching theme of an overburdened life. Because I was permanently affixed, we were never apart, as far as he was concerned. Oh, the mischief I did inside his head. The constant irritation of having to move his thoughts around me to get by me. The desire to eat five hundred French fries without my critical looks. The wish to ogle the tits on every woman without my sneering at him. The way I hid his things when he needed them. Poor baby. No wonder he didn't want to read my chapters. No wonder he didn't want to hear me sing flat. I'd been bugging him all day long:

Don't eat that.

Lower your cholesterol.

Go on a diet.

Get more exercise.

Stop daydreaming.

Pick up your socks.

He couldn't get rid of me. Could I get rid of him?

My office, downstairs from my home, seemed like such a luxury at first. The seven-second commute: descend the spiral staircase and arrive at work. But, like with most things that seem perfect, there were loopholes

More than once, at the bottom of the staircase, my husband ambushed me outside my office door. I think he waited for me there, knowing what would distract me most. We were both masters of ambush and distraction.

I would stab him right before he left for a gig.

He would stab me right before a patient session.

He would speak and black shoe polish would flow from his mouth.

I would tell him he could not go to the birthday party, and then I'd laugh.

And there, on the other side of the door, was Charlene saying, "You're upset. You probably just had a fight with your husband. You know, out of courtesy to me, you shouldn't be doing that, because now that's on your mind when the only thing that should be on your mind is me."

. . .

why I stayed married: **reason #14**

I'D WRITTEN YET another book about couples, and I wanted to have my color photo on the back cover. I'd been looking at other new books that were coming out, and it seemed to me that the more polished the cover, the better the book sold. I wanted this new book, *How to Stay Lovers for Life: Discover a Marriage Counselor's Tricks of the Trade*, to be sold in every airport bookstore. After a long struggle with my publishing house, my feisty editor was getting nowhere. Then one day she called me and said, "Can you do a photo shoot in three hours? We have an author who is getting a color photo, and I got permission to tag you onto the end of the shoot."

At the photo shoot, I was not happy with the way the photographer was posing me, with my hands in my jacket pockets and a smile that declared, "Trust me. This will be the last twenty-two dollars you will ever need to spend on your relationship." As we were shooting, I noticed a huge, blue recycling bin in the corner of the room, and I got an idea. I wanted to call my husband to come over so we could both get photographed inside the recycling bin. We could call the book *Recycling Your Romance*.

My editor said, "Would he *do* that?"

I picked up the phone. My husband was such a good

sport. I knew he'd love the idea of being photographed in a trash can, whether he'd read a page of the book or not.

Getting both of us into the can was not as easy as it looked, and there was the risk of a good topple. After much calculation, he got in first and gently lifted me in facing him. We stood contorted and giggling and smooching and hugging. The photographer snapped and snapped, and we did not notice when he stopped.

chapter 15

I Have No Pet Name for My Vagina

*E*ve drapes herself on my couch, flips off a shoe, and says, "I'm fifty-four years old, and I'm boy-crazy. My pussy is soaked from the moment I wake up until I fall asleep. I glow where the sun don't shine. It's not that I'm worried that I'll walk down my block and fuck a doorman. It's that I'm worried that I'll walk down my block and fuck a doorknob while the doorman is watching. I could put my tongue down some stranger's throat. I could suck off the eighty-year-old Irish man who sells me bread at the green grocer.

"Last night, I stood in front of the mirror and tried on all my tight shirts with no bra underneath," Eve recounts, reliving the moment. "My tits aren't bad. Look, it's my Wonderbra," she points out, rearranging her breasts so they stand and salute. "Then, I masturbated. Then I tried on more tight shirts. Tonight, for a change of pace, I will try on tight pants with no panties underneath. Then I will jerk off again." Eve scrutinizes my body. "You have great tits. Are they real?"

The range of possible therapeutic answers is large:

    a. That came out of left field.
    b. What do you think?
    c. Do you want them to be real?
    d. Should I answer you?
    e. You notice my breasts.
    f. Yes.

Before I can choose an answer, Eve is on to her next thought. "What's worse than hot flashes?" Eve asks, planning to answer herself. "Girly blue balls. Oh, how did I ever refuse a man who had them? I love my little purple people-eater. It takes a licking and keeps on ticking."

Oh, Eve, I think while she speaks, *I can't remember the last time I had a delightful fantasy, let alone a delightful fuck. We both know that a bad marriage can do that. Hell, a good marriage can do that.*

"I devour all my porno e-mail. I keep my mousy clicking, even when I'm not wearing my reading glasses and the photos are so small I can't tell what they are. I wish I'd posed for *Playboy* when I was younger. I wish they'd do a photo spread on women over fifty. I wish I'd fucked more. I wish I hadn't run away when my husband tried to get me to do it with another couple."

"They smell me. Instead of perfume in the morning," she says, moving conspiratorially closer and upending her sentences, "I stick a finger in my pussy and dab each side of my neck. Men love that. When you're that proud—that damn proud of your cunt."

I sit like a stunned deer caught in the headlights on a dark road. Something about the way she crosses and uncrosses her bare legs and offers her breasts like the orange women of Gauguin. Something about the weight of her eyelids smeared like the soft pink of unarticulated promise.

I can smell her neck.

I HAVE NO pet name for my vagina.

My vagina has not occurred to me in years.

I haven't looked.

Or cared.

Maybe it was the antidepressant medication, but I reached a point where it took me three days to masturbate myself to orgasm. On the first two days, I made myself sore. On the third day, like a battered marine, I barely registered a blip on the labia radar screen, at least nothing I even bothered to question. I'd come to consider masturbation a matter of maintaining homeostasis, a biological necessity that occurred while my husband slept in the basement, while I thought about divorce and how I'd afford to keep the house.

I'd lost so many urges—the urge to peek at his cell phone bill, the urge to buy new shoes, the urge to wash my hair. Losing the urge for sex, even for masturbation, was one more time-saver. Maybe I should have written it up and sent it to "Hints From Heloise."

When did I, who had loved touching and being touched so much, shut my body down one zone at a time? How did it happen that I used to love having my nipples caressed, but now the mere thought of it felt like fingernails down a chalkboard? I didn't want another man; nothing man-like got through to me. You could have put me next to a nude Antonio Banderas, and I would have only noticed his accent. I was as numb to cock as if I were six feet under.

It is a strange thing to have so much desire and then—none. When we first met, I remember standing outside my building just before a major hurricane. The air had that dead quality when all hell is about to break loose. We were leaning against a car, kissing, when an old woman from my building walked by us, sneered, and told us to get a room.

Now I knew what she had been thinking, because I was having those thoughts. Crotches stink, fingers stink, feet stink, breath stinks. Spare me.

So, then, I was not passionless, which is the absence of passion. I was passionate about not having sex, not seeing sex, and especially not smelling sex. Movie sex scenes made me as uncomfortable as they had when I was eleven.

There was a big upside to this. When I was boy crazy, I didn't get much done. I certainly didn't write books about love and marriage.

Of course, I had a sexual thing or two I hadn't worked out. It took me decades to tell a therapist what happened to me in the cellar of my house. I had blocked it out, and I'd never put together the consequences, the current impact on my life—why I never could let myself have children, the way I had panic attacks every time I walked upstairs with people behind me, even best friends. I'd never understood why I avoided the 59th Street station on the Lexington Avenue line, where there were so many stairs.

The next week was my birthday. Since I'd been screaming that I wanted a divorce, I knew I wasn't going to have a fancy dinner with my husband. He was too hurt and too angry. I knew that this bout of screaming was different. In the past, we'd been able to put things aside to celebrate, even if only courteously. This time, no such thoughts crossed our minds.

But this was going to be a big, big birthday—I was turning fifty. My friend Karen told me that she'd throw a party for me. The problem was that she lived in Florida, and I didn't know anyone in Florida but Karen. Karen told me I had to come—she was inviting fifty strangers, one for each year of my life. A fiftieth birthday party with fifty strangers? People I'd never, ever met? While I was going through all this shit?

She promised lots of champagne.

So I went off to Florida without my husband, who never would have thought to come to me and say, "I have a surprise. I know how unhappy you've been, so I got us two tickets to Paris. A woman should turn fifty in Paris. Pack light. A woman should buy her birthday dress *for* Paris *in* Paris."

When I got off the plane, Karen told me, "You've gotten dowdy. You used to be so sexy, so cute. You're a frump." She asked me what I planned on wearing to the party, and when I showed her, she threw my black leggings out her porch window and promptly took me to a boutique where she bought me a colorful, slinky little number meant for a samba. I thought I needed a size bigger, but she made me get the smaller size. When we got back to her place, she pulled out her sewing machine and took it in.

I started thinking about the day I took Karen out for her birthday the previous August. On the way out of the restaurant, Karen passed by the very French bartender and said happily, "It's my birthday today." Gallantly, he leaned across the bar and kissed her. I piped in, "It will be my birthday someday, too." He reached over to me and whispered in my ear, "You never have to say that. Just say 'I need to be kissed.'" Then he kissed me. My heart popped like an overstuffed piñata, and every need I'd ever known spilled out. Maybe I could feel sexy again. Maybe I could have sex again. Maybe . . .

Karen was done sewing. I dropped my birthday dress

over my head, complaining it was too tight while she steered me toward the mirror.

Then I caught a glimpse of myself.

Full length.

Front and back.

I was shocked.

Eve was right.

I do have great tits.

●　●　●

why I stayed married: **reason #15**

I WAS IN the bathtub relaxing with an intense thriller. The protagonist had twenty-four hours to find the doomsday plans to stop the doomsday bug (which his girlfriend had contracted) or the whole world could become infected. But now, with three hours left, he was cornered in a European railroad station. Just as he realized there was no way out, the phone in my house rang and startled me.

I accidentally dropped the book in the tub.

It was soaked, unreadable. I put it by the big window, hoping that it might dry out. The next afternoon, when I went to check on it,

a brand new

dry paperback

was sitting in its place.

chapter 16

Fellow Travelers

*I*t is 2:27 p.m.

Charlene is *not* here.

Last week, she showed at 2:22.

The week before, at 2:17.

Her appointment is at 2:00.

This is the same Charlene who always shows up fifteen minutes early, so I know something is up.

Is she late because I don't matter, or is she late because I matter too much?

What she says is, "Ugh, the trains." Or, "Do you know what it's like to get a cab at lunchtime in Midtown?" Or, "Jeez. I forgot." Then she sizes me up—defiantly daring me *not* to buy her story when I know she knows and she knows I know whatever it is we are both pretending not to know.

I mention that a therapy appointment takes emotional labor to forget. It is a tough and sweaty forgetting.

"Oh Sharyn, what do you care? You're getting paid," she says, as if I am a clerk at a 7-Eleven who is thinking about her two-year-old with asthma, who couldn't care less if she sells one more Ding Dong or not.

"This is our time. Every week. Same time. Same place," I remind her again and again.

On our first date, my husband was twenty minutes late. Then he moved back to New York, and, on our third date, he was a few hours late. He lived so far away, it seemed understandable. But by our fifth date, he was twenty-seven and a half hours late, and, from then on, sometimes later than that. The stories piled up. The van broke down. He got a flat tire. He got another flat tire, and this time he had no spare because of the last flat tire. He pulled over to the side of the road to shut his eyes for a few minutes, and it was six hours later when he opened them. I kept trying to be understanding, even though I began to quietly fume.

What was up with all those flat tires? I drove a car. I knew how many flat tires to expect in a year. How was I able to create the rationale for him that, as a starving artist, he must be buying cheap retreads that didn't hold up? This, when I could find no rationale from Charlene satisfactory. I only saw Charlene 2,250 minutes a year, and spent a number of those minutes puzzled about her lateness, but I never thought about understanding his. It must have taken emotional labor to ignore. It must have been a tough and sweaty forgetting.

"Charlene, what should I do when I'm waiting for you?"

"Jeez, can we stop this? It's a great time for you to catch up on your reading. I mean, you are reading up on my case, aren't you?"

I hate sitting and waiting for a patient. I feel dumped. Later, they say, "I was going to call from the subway platform, but my cell phone doesn't get reception," or, "I meant to call, I really did. I don't know why I didn't." I hated sitting and waiting for my husband. He'd call to tell me he'd be late one hour *after* he was supposed to have arrived. I'd be all dressed up. I'd spend hours getting ready to wait. Eventually, I learned to take whatever he told me would be his arrival time and add hours and hours to it. I learned many ways to pass the hours.

I learned to feel hurt.

I learned to feel furious.

I learned to feel desperate.

I learned to eat a pint of Ben & Jerry's.

I learned to feel like throwing up.

I learned to yell.

I learned to become hysterical.

I learned to fall asleep by the window in an upright position wearing silvery tap pants and lipstick.

But I never learned to ask the simple question: What is his message to me?

How did I let this go on for so many years without asking this question? What was I willing to put myself through for him?

Charlene is saying, "I hate this therapist shit."

"What do you hate most about it?"

"I have important things to discuss. Can we stop this, please?"

"Your behavior is drowning out your words."

Charlene and I go back and forth. She continues to be late. She never answers my questions about it. I never let up. Will we still be doing this fifteen years from now?

Fifteen years ago, in the very beginning, he said, "I had a flat tire, and someone stole my jack. I had to wait until someone stopped."

"Oh my God," I answered. "That sounds awful. It's a hundred degrees outside. You must have really started to get worried. Are you OK now?"

"I'm exhausted. So I'm gonna stay in a motel in Connecticut tonight, and I'll see you tomorrow morning at ten."

At ten the next morning, the coffee was on. At ten thirty, the coffee was warming. At eleven, my phone rang.

"There was a party in the room next to me. Music all night. I just woke up. I'm gonna jump in the shower. I'll be there around one thirty. See ya then. Bye."

Was it a month, two months, into the relationship when I started to become his mother? "Check the tires before you go. Make sure you bring your license and your registration. Stop for coffee. Call me when you stop." It made me hate myself, besides which it never worked. He never got to my house even one minute earlier.

It is 2:33 p.m. My husband—I mean Charlene—has just arrived. Her session will be over in twelve minutes. She barrels in flustered, her perfume overpowering the room. Her tangled leopard scarf and the pink raincoat that she throws on the couch waft with Charlene until it is almost like I'm not there. How am I supposed to comment on her being late when she is vibrating, promising to explode? Her presence is so large, there's no me there at all. She is the twenty-four-hour news station on the radio: All Charlene. All the time.

I have a memory of an early session years ago when Charlene told me that sitting in a room with her mother was like being a gnat behind a plant in the corner. Her mother was so expansive, so huge and looming, that Charlene felt reduced, annihilated—but not quite. Not quite, because her mother required her to witness. Suddenly, I understand what is happening between us: I am playing little Charlene, the insubstantial gnat behind the plant in the corner. I am to experience all the feelings that Charlene experienced from the mammoth mother. She is helping me to understand what words cannot convey—the frustration, the anger, the rejection. I am supposed to save Charlene from spending her life in the corner and from turning into her mother. She is showing me instead of telling me what we are supposed to do together.

I say, "What do you imagine our time together would

have been like if you'd been here on time?" My voice is warmer.

She begins to tell me what her life would be like if anyone cared, if anyone listened, if anyone made time and room for her. She softens.

I try to imagine what my relationship with my husband would have been like if he had come to me on time. Maybe he was avoiding the contact, the dependency (his or mine), my frustration, or even my love. It would be easy to focus on him.

But what was I doing?

This is a question I've been trying to answer for years— every time a friend told me that he and I didn't even seem married.

Today I realize that, in order to understand what kept us together, I would have had to do what I finally did: leave him. Then I could begin to see that we stayed together so long because we had so much in common—the last good time in each of our lives happened before we hit the age of three. We were joined in holy matrimony to suffer. We had found so many ways to do it. We'd never get bored. We were so compatible.

Early on, when it seemed that all I did was sit by the window waiting, when it seemed that all he did was over-sleep or forget to change his oil, we were actually staking out the perimeter of our drama. My part was to believe that if I suffered properly and long enough he'd show up on time. I suffered when he did not. His part was to hope that when he showed up late I would forgive him. He suffered when I did not.

In fact, he suffered for the entire 217-mile drive from New York to Boston because he knew what was coming. Naturally, his suffering never got him to leave earlier the next time. This was not the point. But his suffering did make him pull over in a rest stop on the turnpike and fall asleep as my suffering did get me to press the phone to my chest as if it were my failing newborn.

Together, we sought out suffering and hoped for love. The job of love wasn't to get us past suffering. The job of love was to suffer. That was all we knew. So you can see how lucky we were, that out of all the people in the world, we'd found each other.

As fellow travelers, we joined in matrimony to love our pain, to honor our losses, to obey our torment. Huge disappointments till death do us part.

•   •   •

why I stayed married: **reason #16**

WE HAD PLANNED a vacation to New Hampshire where we would hike the White Mountains and visit Nathaniel Hawthorne's flume. The car was packed with more provisions than any two people could need on a vacation, plus one upright bass—just in case.

Two hours into the trip, we pulled off the highway into a small town to find a much-needed cup of decent coffee. We both spotted a little java joint with a green, hand-painted sign that looked like it would deliver the goods.

While I was waiting for my husband to return to the table with the drinks, I leafed through a local paper and saw a photo of a stately, gargantuan moose. When my husband returned, before he could even sit down, I excitedly announced, "I want to see a moose on our vacation." He was not sure that the White Mountains would provide such a treat, but I repeated like a spoiled child, "I need to see a moose. I am not coming home till I see one."

He looked at the article and saw it was about Moosehead Lake in Maine, where, not surprisingly, moose abound and it was calving time. He pulled out his cell phone and began making calls. Within thirty minutes, we were cancelled out of New Hampshire and rerouted to Moosehead Lake. The flume would have to wait.

That very night, he managed to hire us a private moose safari, where, from a canoe on a still river, we gleefully watched a bull moose bellow as a cow tended her two calves, and the white-tailed deer made the strangest hollers we'd ever heard.

chapter 17

The Last-Ditch Attempt

"Umm. I'm not coming back to therapy," Lisa informs me as she stands at the door, getting ready to leave. "I decided to spend the money on a weekly massage. I can use that more than this."

This is Lisa, I think, Lisa who has come every week for eighty-three weeks.

"Shouldn't we have a proper good-bye?" I ask.

This is no proper good-bye. This is no retrospective of the work we've done, the work left to do. This is no respectful parting where we don't want to end, but it's time—where we both get to say what we need to say.

This is not nice.

This is a giant Fuck You.

Lisa smiles sweetly, turns in a way that would make Giselle jealous, and dances out the door.

I am getting dumped for a shoulder rub!

Lisa, don't you remember when you came to see me because your husband kept singing, "Lisa, Lisa, with the meatball eyes," and you couldn't stand it? Remember how he kept buying you Kleenex and toilet paper until you ran out of closet space, but he couldn't say, "I love you"? Remember how you fought after every social occasion? I helped you with all that.

I know good-byes are hard, but why this way?

Did you think I would try to talk you out of leaving therapy just because I would have tried to talk you out of leaving therapy?

Did you even give it a second thought?

Did you fall out of love with me and forget to tell me about it?

Meanwhile, I've fallen out of love with my husband, and I'm waiting like a consumptive field mouse for him to be ambushed with divorce papers. I call the lawyer on the sly, telling her when he'll be home and when I won't.

"Let's surprise him at work," she says. "That way we know he'll be there."

I refuse, in spite of the glee in her voice. I would never embarrass him on the bandstand that way. I cannot believe she suggests it.

"Hardball," she says. "We're playing hardball."

We finally settle on a time when I will be visiting a friend, and he'll still be sleeping. When I hang up, I am shaking with worry, with fear, with disbelief. I can't stop thinking about our marriage. My head becomes a walking VCR as the videos of our relationship play over and over again—Italy in spring, boxes all over the house, Milton Nascimento, the night he started speeding while we were fighting in the car and half scared me to death.

When I was falling out of love with my husband, I told him about it. I was the sports announcer giving blow-by-blow coverage: *The marriage is shaky. The wife is roaring. The husband appears to be hurt. The marriage is down for the count.*

In fact, I told too much. I talked about it daily. In doing so, I made him immune. I now think that talking about it daily is exactly the same as saying nothing at all.

Lisa, our therapy went up and down like any other therapy. I know that I can have an edge, and that sometimes I said things you didn't want to hear. Is that why you left? Do you have resentment that I never knew about?

I have so much resentment. I once thought that I could fix my marriage by going on vacations—so we went everywhere. I thought I could fix my marriage by fixing myself. I worked so hard on myself because I thought that marriage would make me a better person. I did all the things I told my patients to do. It worked for a while, and working on myself made me love my husband more. I changed the way I thought about so many things.

For the things I could not change, I went on antidepressants. For just the few wee, unchangeable things left, I increased my dose. The marriage got better still.

When Lisa was depressed in her marriage and in her life, I sent her for an evaluation for antidepressant medication. Her marriage got better, too. She found a way to be grateful for all the extra Kleenex, all the toilet paper. When she became grateful instead of angry, her husband no longer needed to walk in the house with ten rolls of Scott tissue placed as armor against his chest. He was able to relieve the anxiety that led him to stuff the cabinets. Lisa relaxed, too. Her husband became less obsessed with running out of toilet paper. They began to hold hands. The toilet paper actually became a funny story to tell at a dinner party.

When I put both my feet in the door and increased my antidepressants for the few little things falling out of my head, the marriage got much better for a while. I didn't mind the big, messy piles my husband left everywhere, or the fact that he could never get his taxes in on time or pay off his debt, which seemed to grow in leaps and bounds. I was happy. And he was happy, too. The house filled with piles, the garbage overflowed, my husband worked seven nights and seven days a week, and the debt grew and grew. The piles became funny stories to tell at dinner parties.

Except we never went to any.

Next, I gave Lisa twenty-five marriage-saving tips to dissolve fights. For example, her husband had a big mouth.

Whenever they went to a party, he'd divulge something that made her furious. He mentioned her preoccupation with liposuction, his theories about her relationship with her tap dance teacher, the family finances. Every party turned into a battlefield in the cab home. The cab ride there was no better. Lisa would spend it all tensed up, wanting to remind him over and over again not to do what he always did, but too anxious to actually say anything.

What he always did. Clearly, this was a clue, I suggested to Lisa. Why wait until the cab ride home to fight? Why not start the fight on the cab ride there? Since his big mouth is a sure thing, just get it over with.

My husband never said anything that embarrassed me at a party. Why? I could never get him *to* the party. On the way to Sally's Yom Kippur breakfast, he started a huge fight in the car about how long we'd stay. After we parked the car and started walking toward her apartment, he stomped off, leaving me alone. On the way to Frank's for drinks, he said he couldn't go because he'd decided that I was oppressive and keeping him from his work. Even worse was the first party we threw—and I say *we* loosely because it was *I and I only* who threw it. We'd been together for thirteen years and he still wasn't ready to have a party. So, I rented a space out of the house, hired people to cook and clean up, and invited fifty people.

Then we moved into our new home. For one year, we fought about having a party. "No, no, no, no, no," he said to seventeen potential dates. Finally, I chose one, announced it, and began to invite people. "This is not my party," he told me, "and I'm not doing anything for it. I may not even show up." And a few days later, "You can't torment me this way. You can't bully me this way." I bought food and cooked for sixty people. I sent him off for soda, and he grumbled nonstop. I made vegetarian chili and corn bread and tomatoes with buffalo mozzarella. He said I chose to make the chili, which took so long to cook, just to torment him. I think I tore my rotator cuff stirring the corn bread.

Lisa said, "We're having so much fun. Last week, we went to a party. In the cab on the way there, I yelled at him for things he hasn't done yet. He apologized and stuck his hand up my dress. We're having great sex. And we decided to take your advice about the vacations. Last weekend, I had the best orgasm I've ever had. And, you won't believe this— we're going to a yoga retreat in Thailand. That thing you said about two big vacations a year and four weekends. Well, we've already planned the year out. Next weekend, we're going to a New Jersey Hilton. Room service, sex, a Jacuzzi, pay-per-view movies in the room. We are going to eat, eat, eat and fuck, fuck, fuck."

My husband and I used to take vacations. But in the last two years, we had stopped. "I'm overwhelmed. I have seventeen gigs in twelve days. I can't go anywhere," he'd say.

When I finally got him to the west coast of Florida to visit my folks, he brought his laptop.

I ate breakfast on the beach in the morning.

He stayed in the guest bedroom. "Don't bother me now.

I have to get this done."

I went to the fishing pier to watch the dolphins feed in the afternoon.

He was still in the bedroom on the laptop. "Don't bother me now. I'm at a critical time."

I slept on the beach one night watching a sea turtle nest.

"Have a good time, but leave me alone. I don't want to be here. I told you that." He sat inside with the laptop, furiously typing.

But . . . based on what Lisa said, I decided to try one final marriage-rescue intervention—like when they come and capture your teenager on drugs and take her away.

We were sitting with the shrink, who was to be our sixth and final couple's therapist. My close friend Alexia had just died after a long bout with cancer. I was inconsolable, and I decided that I should do something that I had always wanted to do—in her honor—and what I had always wanted to do was go to a rainforest. In a last-ditch effort, I said to my husband, "Go to Costa Rica with me. We've always had great vacations. We'll see wild monkeys. I want you to come."

"I can't get away. I don't know how you could ask me now."

"I'm going to go alone, then."

"You can't do that. It isn't appropriate."

"Appropriate? We're on the verge of a divorce."

"OK. I'll go."

I bought the tickets.

I paid for the hotel room in advance.

A few days before we were scheduled to leave, we were back in the therapist's office, and my husband said, "I'm not going. Too much work." He said that he'd spent the marriage doing what I wanted when I wanted. He was going to take care of himself now and not be bullied.

The therapist said, "I'd be cautious about making that choice right now. Your marriage is on the line. If you don't go, you'll likely have made the choice to end the marriage."

My husband said, "I know."

Finally, he agreed to meet me in Costa Rica over the weekend.

But he never showed up.

My advice to Lisa worked. Her marriage got better and better and better, and then she didn't need me at all.

Mine got worse and worse and worse.

One day when I was seeing my own therapist, my husband answered the door and was served divorce papers. He was furious when I came home—outraged, actually. He told me I'd served him divorce papers at the worst possible time. A couple of weeks passed, and I received his counter-complaint. He, too, sued me for cruel and abusive treatment—for humiliations above and beyond. He cited them: The time I forced him to go to Florida. The time I forced him to have a party. The time I locked myself out of the house and insisted he leave work and let me in.

So, the paperwork is done.

It's all in motion.

Lisa is off getting massages and being happy.

If I weren't so anxious, I'd be happier, too.

I might need surgery on my rotator cuff from stirring the corn bread.

. . .

why I stayed married: **reason #17**

I LIKE TO eat a slice of bread before bed every single night. In fact, I can't sleep if I don't. More than once, my husband had run to the market at midnight when we'd run out of bread.

One week, I was flying off on a thirteen-city book tour— from Boston to Los Angeles with city after city in between. I was nervous and I knew I'd be exhausted by the schedule. I didn't know how I was going to manage thirteen cities in fifteen days.

When I arrived in my Boston hotel room, I was already tired. I dropped my heavy bags in a chair and flopped on the bed and then I saw it: there, next to the television, was an ornate silver platter with a single slice of bread on it.

chapter 18

Peeling a Marriage

*T*he couple sits in mediation, peeling a marriage—the layers of who did what to the
layers of who gets what to the layers of who
pays what to the layers of who failed whom.

The husband asks, "Is this a place where we can talk, if
we want to, about the relationship?"

He wants to talk. There is something he wants her to
understand that he believes she cannot understand. He
thinks that if he says the right words, or just enough words,
she will get it. He tries different combinations but gets
nowhere.

Just as their agendas for the meetings are different, their

preparations for these meetings are different, too. He prepares by making computer printouts—financial charts, spreadsheets, long lists that can be added, subtracted, divided. Perhaps he imagines he can find the root, that the critical incident can be pinpointed with numbers.

"It's all in the data," he says with certainty. "It doesn't matter what you *feel*. Look at the numbers. The numbers never lie."

Her method is to sit on the living room couch and stare at the shoe polish on the couch skirt. She recalls the helpless feeling of watching their expensive couch get its stripes.

In the light of fifteen years together, is this what it comes down to? Scuff marks? She searches for the fury she needs to face another mediation session. She is afraid that if she goes in with less than that, she will fold within minutes.

In the first hour and a half of mediation, he presents, whipping pages out of a briefcase, while furiously entering new data into the laptop that serves as an emotional bullet-proof vest. He avoids direct eye contact, talks almost continually, explains that every detail must be discussed and he will not be rushed. In the last half hour of mediation, he tells her he can't believe what she has done to him. He is sleeping at a friend's house on an unheated basement floor. He chokes up when he asks about the dogs.

In the first hour and a half of mediation, she sits with the man she can't be with anymore, the man who wants all the retirement money, the man who never got around to filing their taxes for two years, the man who stood her up in Costa Rica. But in the last half hour of every session, she sits with the boy with the shoe in his hand, the handsome jazz musician on the concert stage, the man who danced her across the living room to the theme song from *Beauty and the Beast.*

We are a couple made of pieces and parts. Our marriage is like a paint-by-numbers horse. And our little lives are rounded with a separation agreement. These are the kinds of phrases she conjures up as she sits there. She is writing a book. She is seeking a nice turn of phrase to capture agony. It is the only exercise that keeps her from believing the things that his pure pain is telling her about herself.

When a meeting ends, she runs to the elevator, hoping that it will take him a few minutes to pack up his papers so she won't have to ride down with him. Or, she dawdles, hoping to get an extra minute with him. It varies from week to week. Then she goes home to the home they made together—the home that, bit by bit, she is erasing him from. She erases him from the bathroom cabinet, tossing out shaving cream, full bottles of aftershave, athlete's foot cream. She erases him from the Con Ed bill, changing the name on the billing address. She erases him from the bedroom, carrying his boxes into the basement, emptying his errant socks into a Hefty bag, buying all new pillows. Even the dogs can barely smell him anymore.

In her foolish belief that throwing away his things could ever make him go away, she suddenly realizes that she has only a few minutes to change gear from a woman who doesn't know how she will manage to get through this financial, emotional, and physical fiasco to a therapist who has to help others through their financial, emotional, and physical fiascos. In the end, the transition is never quite complete. She is afraid they will catch on. She bites the inside of her lip, says she needs a glass of water, takes off a shoe and rubs her foot on the rug—anything to keep her out of her head and in the sessions with her patients.

Soon, it all clicks in as they transport her far, far away from her mess into their mess. What would she do without them? If they are one minute late, she gets scared. She goes to the window and looks out, then runs back into her office when she sees them coming so they won't know how much she needs them.

Her patients count on her to help them while the truth is that she needs them as much as they need her. She needs them desperately. She wilts like a hungry sunflower waiting for her little watering cans. When they revive her, she will be able to take care of everything, of them all, of herself—she will be able to process her mediation session. She will even be able to go back to living and speaking in the singular, in the first person.

·   ·   ·

why I stayed married: **reason #18**

It is 10 p.m. and my best friend from the sixth grade, Donna, and I are sitting at the bar in the Westin Hotel in downtown Boston. There is a jazz trio playing, and the bass player is cute in his black tuxedo and red bow tie. This is our third stop of the evening. We are loose and happy. We know the name of every bartender in all three clubs. Donna eyes the red bow tie, and says, "I want him. I'm talking altar."

I know what to do to help her get him. It's a two-part plan. First, we request a song that shows that we know jazz. Donna suggests "New York, New York," which I quickly veto in favor of the lush Ellington tune, "Prelude to a Kiss."

I rise slowly and approach the bandstand. Though I speak to them all, the bass player is the only one who looks up. I make the request. The bass player begins to play the tune all by himself, his fingers moving up and down the neck of the double bass with speed and authority. I watch his strong, flat fingers with wonder. The band never joins in, so he finishes the tune alone.

Back at our table, I order a round of drinks for the band—whatever they want. When they hit the last chord of the fast 4/4 blues that signals their break, they come over to our table cradling their Courvoisier. The red bow tie sits down and talks in a voice that sounds as if he gargles pebbles.

Donna is flirting, and I am not. She is a much better flirt, but she fails to recognize my one great advantage: I have no day job. I could hang out till the end of the night—longer even. More importantly, I recognize that you never win a musician by requesting "New York, New York."

As we talk to the red bow tie, we find out he lives in New York City in the East Village, and he plays with Ron Carter. He travels to Japan and Brazil. He plays at the Village Vanguard.

I've always wanted to go to the Village Vanguard. I've always wanted to live in New York City. I think I should have him, not Donna.

I have one other advantage: I'm a singer. In fact, I know the piano player in the trio from before. Because of the top-shelf drink, he remembers me like it was yesterday, and he invites me to sit in.

This begins the story that he and I will tell others over and over again through the fifteen years to come:

I swear that I sang "When I Fall in Love," and then I did.

He swears that I sang "Stormy Weather," and then it was.

Epilogue

*I*t is a cool and glorious summer morning. I have made plans with my friend Victoria to have a French brunch. A rich French brunch is not my first choice, but Victoria is very glamorous, and I always enjoy myself with her—and I'm especially tickled by what she wears. She's in the fashion business, and she has saved every Moschino jacket since the sixties. It's always a treat to see how she puts herself together, and I've learned a thing or two from her.

I decide to walk through the neighborhood to the restaurant and do a bit of visiting on the way. I make a quick stop at Barnes & Noble to say hello to Cynthia, who put my last book on display. Then I visit her competitor, Kizmin, who owns Partners & Crime, a mystery bookstore less than a block away. I always wanted to work at a bookstore, but the money was so bad. Once, when I told Kizmin, she offered me a part-time job getting paid in books instead of cash—a paperback an hour, a trade paperback for two hours, a new hardcover for three hours. I only worked on Sundays, but it was nirvana to tidy stacks and discover new authors and take them home. My bedside table was overflowing with spies and serial killers and my favorite whodunits. Plus, it was extremely rewarding to recommend a book and have the patron return the next week to buy five more of my recommendations.

As I leave the bookstore, I realize it is hotter than I'd thought, so I stop to buy an overpriced bottle of water and slug it down. I touch my hair, which is soaked, and I trickle a little water on my forehead to try and cool off.

Walking toward the restaurant, I discover that this is the day of the big gay pride parade. How can I complain about being hot when the sidewalk is overflowing with folk decked out in festive drag, their foundation bubbling under the sun?

I am taking in the rainbow of people when I hear an unmistakable voice call my name. What? Huh? I literally I bump into the man I was married to—outside of a small jazz club where he must be taking a break from playing bass at the brunch.

It's been a year and a half since I've seen him. Screw Hollywood and those scenes of poignant meetings years later like the ones in *The Way We Were* and *Splendor in the Grass*. Screw Barbra Streisand and Natalie Wood and Robert Redford and Warren Beatty. Their movies have not left me well prepared.

He wears a pale blue, rayon-blend shirt that's nicer and

neater than any shirt he ever wore while we were married, and tan pants like the ones I'd always wished he'd buy but never did. In fact, now that I've mentioned it, I think he is wearing the tan pants I bought him five or six holidays ago, the pants he never bothered to get shortened.

I say, "Hello . . ."

He nods.

We, who could not stop yelling at each other, stand mute in the middle of the parade.

"How are the dogs?" he asks finally.

"Should I leave them to you in my will?" I respond stupidly.

"Are you sick or is this a hypothetical question?" he asks me.

I babble, "I love them. I can't live without them. When they go, I go."

He gazes off at some place out there I cannot see and says, "Once, you said the same things about me."

He looks real good in the blue shirt.

I'm not ready for this surprise reunion. I am not ready to see the man I used to love and kind of still do. He was family, and so I thought this marriage was supposed to last forever, and we could take care of each other and find enough ways to be happy.

Instead, our marriage was awash with our childhood injuries—all the pain that children are never meant to feel, but so often do. We were unable to plow through it. I don't know why.

I don't know why so many of my patients got better when we could not.

Still, on most days, I am happier in my heartbreak than I was before.

"How are you?" I ask, really meaning it.

He hesitates, and I feel an old tug.

There are so many reasons to celebrate.

But I am in the middle of a parade on my way to a French brunch.

There are croissants and café au lait and rich surprises and my friend Victoria waiting for me.

And there is something else—even more importantly—there is something else.

•   •   •

why I left my husband: **reason #1**

NONE OF THE reasons to stay were enough.